# REFLECTIONS OF
# Hartwood

*by Jeffrey S. Lawrence*

NOTE: Where "Recollections of
Hartwood" is referenced,
the author is Victor E. Robb

# Table of Contents

# Preface

In 2005 my dad, John W. Lawrence Jr. (Johnny as he was known as a child or J.W. as he was known in later years), and I were in the process of getting some of our 18mm home movies converted into DVD format. We were very surprised when one specific video came back from the development company. It showed John and Mary Flinn Lawrence's wedding video that was shot on their wedding day: June 11, 1914—over 100 years ago. We were excited to see such an amazing video, and this video is really what started me on my journey to compile family videos, photos and later recorded interviews with people that had a connection to Hartwood.

Every so often, Dad would call and tell me that he had a photo of "this" or a document showing "that" for my files—he called me the "Official Family Archivist." I would catalog everything into several piles and put it into my personal library. After a few years of compiling and cataloging material, the thought occurred to me that I might just have enough information to write a book about Hartwood. Initially, Dad balked at the idea as he was a very private person. I explained to Dad that the book would be about our family history as well as the Hartwood buildings and grounds, and mainly for the enjoyment of the thousands of visitors that Hartwood attracts every year. Once Dad realized that the book would be a written celebration of Hartwood, he eventually came on board with the idea for the book.

On September 25, 2007, Dad and I walked through the mansion and grounds with a hand-held tape recorder as he recorded his thoughts and recollections about growing up in such a magnificent house and estate. Some of his stories I had heard a hundred times—those of you who knew J.W. know what I am talking about! Other stories I heard for the first time. As I transcribed that audio tape I could hear the emotion in his voice while he described what each room in the mansion meant to him and what the people were like that worked and lived at Hartwood.

My motivation for writing this book is to share the resources and documents that I have accumulated. These videos, photos, and documents are to be shared in the form of this book with the people who love Hartwood. They would not do anyone any good just sitting in my library collecting dust. Allegheny County will own Hartwood for countless years to come; I believe that this wonderful "Jewel of Allegheny County" deserves an accurate and fitting written history.

I hope you enjoy this book as much as I enjoyed collecting all of these wonderful reflections....

"It is too bad that a requirement for living is not leaving a record of it."
—Lynda Rutledge Stephenson

# Acknowledgements

I would like to dedicate this book to my father, John W. Lawrence Jr. During the many hours I spent reading, researching, and compiling this book many memories resurfaced of my Dad and his thoughts and stories about growing up at Hartwood. Dad was truly a one-of-a-kind individual and is deeply missed by family and friends. I dedicate this book to you, Dad. He (as he described himself) was "the best friend that Hartwood ever had."

My wife Kim and my daughter Hannah would endure my disappearing into my office for hours on end, where I was typing away on my laptop. I thank them for being understanding of my many recorded phone conversations for the book and my many trips to Hartwood (I need just one more photo!), and many hours of not being with them while working on this book. It was a sacrifice that they made for me, for which I am eternally grateful, and words cannot express my thanks.

A big thank you goes out to Hartwood park managers Linda Joy and Patti Benaglio. I have had the joy to personally work with each of these fine women for years now. Each was just a phone call or an email away. They (along with the docents) truly love Hartwood and the history and they were very gracious with their time and knowledge. I thank each of you from the bottom of my heart.

After some articles were published in the Pittsburgh area about this project, I was contacted by many people that either lived or worked at Hartwood. I cannot thank each and every one of you enough for the opportunity to interview each person and to really get a feel for the way Hartwood was back in the day. Each person gave so much of themselves and their time to help me in the endeavor that I truly appreciate it. Your dedication and thoughtfulness has not gone unnoticed—thank you!

## FRIENDS OF HARTWOOD

A hearty thank you goes out to my many friends at the Friends of Hartwood (both past and present). They were a wonderful resource for me—with countless emails, phone calls, and questions asked. Please financially contribute to this wonderful organization as they raise money for various projects around Hartwood. Visit their interactive website at www.friendsofhartwood.org to learn more about this great group of people that truly love Hartwood. Make sure to attend their largest fund raiser of the year, Hartwood Fest, held in the fall at the stable complex at Hartwood. Lots of food, fun, hayrides, and a huge bonfire—it's a great time.

Hartwood Mansion
200 Hartwood Acres (off Saxonburg Blvd.)
Hampton Township, PA 15238
Phone 412-767-9200 / Fax 412-767-0171

# Pennsylvania Senator and Mogul William Flinn

Portrait of Senator William Flinn. Photo courtesy of Hartwood archives.

Before we can begin any discussion of the grandeur of Hartwood or how Hartwood came to be, we must first discuss Mary Flinn Lawrence's father: Senator William Flinn—because without Senator Flinn there would not have been a Hartwood.

Senator Flinn's life and career are really a story about how an immigrant that started out with nothing became a force not only in industry but in politics as well. Through sheer hard work and determination (as well as some street-smarts), William Flinn became a true, self-made American success story.

William Flinn was born on May 26, 1851 in Manchester, England to John and Mary (Hamilton) Flinn; parents of Irish descent who raised the family Roman Catholic. The other Flinn siblings were two sons Charles Emmet Flinn and Phillip S. Flinn as well as a daughter, Katherine Flinn. The Flinn family sought refuge in England due to political turmoil in Ireland and to seek a better life for their four children. The Flinns immigrated to eastern PA after they arrived in New York (when William was one year old). Shortly thereafter, the family moved to the Pittsburgh, PA area to make their home.

The family moved to the old sixth ward in Pittsburgh, where young William left public school at the tender age of nine to help support the family. He shined shoes and later sold newspapers. In his teenage years he entered into the apprenticeship program to become a brass finisher and a steamfitter, which was followed by being a journeyman for three years. It was about this time that the young William Flinn started his own construction company. William's father had also owned a small construction firm; he passed away when William was in his early teens. It is said that the young William Flinn started out with some shovels, work carts, a few men, and dogged determination. Through hard work William grew his small company into a firm that would build many public works projects in the Pittsburgh, PA area and later in the New York, NY area.

In 1874 William Flinn married Butler, PA native Nancy Galbraith (July 20, 1851 – April 27, 1927). William and Nancy soon started a family of which seven children were born to them; they are listed here in order of birth: George H. (1875-1929), Ralph Emerson (1876-1949), Howard G. (1876-1879), William Arthur (1881-1964), Alexander Rex (1886-1950), Mary Stephen (1887-1974), and Edith (1889-1961).

Nancy Galbraith Flinn and Senator William Flinn. Photo is not dated and is courtesy of Hartwood archives.

Nancy Galbraith Flinn. Photo is not dated and is courtesy of Hartwood archives.

Undated photo of Nancy Galbraith Flinn from family home movies courtesy of the author.

Flinn started his construction business in 1876 when he was 25 years old. In 1877 he merged his small general contracting firm with the firm of a competitor owned by James J. Booth. This new partnership was known as Booth and Flinn Construction Company, with Flinn being the junior partner. It has been said that the young firm's first contract was grading, paving, and installing curbing and sewers in Pittsburgh's streets.

It was around this time that the young William Flinn began a lifelong interest (and later career) in politics. In 1877, at the age of twenty six, he was elected to the Pittsburgh Board of Fire Commissioners—the first of many political positions that Flinn would hold and a very influential political post at that time. It was also the only municipal office that he would ever hold. Flinn entered into one of his first (and definitely not his last) political frays while investigating fraud at the ballot box. Flinn's brother Charles E.

Flinn and several other prominent citizens voted for a particular candidate, and when the votes were counted at the polling place they were returned for that candidate as having received no votes. William Flinn instigated the investigation and found that votes were tampered with. Prosecutions soon followed, and William Flinn gained a reputation as someone who was no-nonsense and honest.

Early portrait of William Flinn, around the time he started Booth and Flinn Construction. Photo courtesy of Hartwood archives.

In the late 1870's William Flinn became friends and developed an alliance with another political up-and-comer in the Allegheny County area, Christopher Lyman Magee. Both staunch supporters of the Republican Party, the Pittsburgh political machine of Magee and Flinn was born, each boss controlling their respective sections of Pittsburgh for the next 20 years.

The landmark 1903 book by Lincoln Steffens titled *The Shame of the Cities* detailed the political graft and corruption of the Flinn-Magee partnership:

*"A happy, profitable combination, it lasted for life. Magee wanted power, Flinn wealth. Each got both these things; but Magee spent his wealth for more power, and Flinn spent his power for more wealth. Magee was the sower, Flinn the reaper. In dealing with men they became necessary to each other, these two. Magee attracted followers, Flinn employed them."*

Early photo of "Boss" Bill Flinn. Photo courtesy of Hartwood archives.

In addition to young William Flinn's rising political star status, Booth and Flinn's contracts exceeded $4 million annually during this same time period. Flinn's political career at the Pittsburgh level began to come to a close in the late 1890's due to a political fight with Edward Bigelow, Director of Public Works in Pittsburgh, concerning accusations of the rigged bidding system; this bidding system is how Booth and Flinn secured contracts for the city of Pittsburgh's public works projects. On one occasion Booth and Flinn bid $31,500 to provide Ligoner paver block for the new Public Safety Building. Another firm bid $18,000. The contract was later revised to require that the block be a certain shade of bluish tint rather than the standard grey variety found in this type of block. Only the block from a certain Booth-and-Flinn-owned quarry contained that certain bluish tint required for the contract.

In the Western Pennsylvania area, noteworthy projects built by Booth and Flinn include the Liberty Tunnels, the George Westinghouse Memorial Bridge (1931), the Jacks Run Bridge in Pittsburgh, along with building several miles of the Pennsylvania Turnpike. In 1929 Booth and Flinn Construction was awarded a contract to build the five-mile-long Ohio River Boulevard along with nine bridges of considerable size; this was among the largest single road and bridge building contracts ever awarded to a firm by the Pittsburgh District. Booth and Flinn also installed most of the streetcar lines installed in Pittsburgh between 1895 and 1910. When Johnstown, PA was hit with a devastating flood in 1889 the company sent several thousand workers to this hard-hit town to help with rescue work and the cleanup effort.

In 1898 when senior partner James J. Booth retired from the firm, eldest son George H. Flinn took over the reins at Booth and Flinn Construction. In 1909 William Flinn bought out Booth at a cost of $2,000,000, thus transferring full control of the company to the Flinn family. Flinn's two other sons, A. Rex Flinn and William Flinn, then joined the firm in 1924. Son Ralph Emerson Flinn also worked at the firm. The firm established a satellite office in the New York City area sometime in the late 1920's; George H. Flinn ran that office until his untimely death on March 29, 1929. George's brother A. Rex Flinn then assumed control. Booth and Flinn existed as a company until the late 1950's when it was sold to a private interest.

Through the competitive bidding process Booth and Flinn received contracts to build the Holland Tunnel connecting New York City and New Jersey. When this contract for $23,000,000 was awarded in 1922, it was at that time the largest contract ever awarded to a single construction company in the United States.

Political caricature of Senator Flinn dated October 1900. The Senator is sitting atop the Pittsburgh City Hall building. Courtesy of Hartwood archives.

In 1879 and again in 1881 William Flinn was elected to the State House of Representatives. About the time Flinn was beginning his career as a political boss in Pittsburgh, he was elected the Republican chairman of the city executive committee in 1882 and held that chair until 1899. In 1888 Flinn attended the Republican national convention as a delegate. In 1890 Flinn was elected to the PA state Senate representing the 44th District, where he sponsored the Good Roads Act, which became law in 1895. Flinn was re-elected to his Senate post again in 1894 as well as 1898, resigning from the Senate on March 7, 1901. From 1884 until 1912 Senator Flinn was appointed a delegate to every Republican National convention.

In May of 1912 Flinn was elected chairman of the State's Republican Party; however, Flinn held this post for only two months. In July of 1912 the Senator's political leanings turned to the Progressive Party as there was political infighting between the Republican Party and Roosevelt's newly formed Progressive "Bull Moose" Party. This new upstart party was headed by Teddy Roosevelt, with whom Flinn was close personal friends and shared political views. The Progressive Party was started in 1912 by Colonel Roosevelt after he had a falling out with the Republican Party and President Taft. Flinn was upset that the Republicans did not nominate Roosevelt to be their candidate in the 1912 presidential campaign; they instead chose incumbent President William Howard Taft. Senator Flinn was instrumental in helping Colonel Roosevelt win Pennsylvania. Senator Flinn remained active in the Progressive Party until it was dissolved in 1916.

The following account was printed in a local newspaper at the time of Senator Flinn's passing, and it details the political respect between Colonel Roosevelt and Senator Flinn. The name of the newspaper and publish date of the article is unknown.

## Roosevelt on Flinn

Theodore Roosevelt, speaking at Tucson, Arizona on September 17, 1912, paid an emphatic tribute to the service rendered by William Flinn to the Progressive cause. While Roosevelt was speaking someone in the crowd yelled out: *"What about Bill Flinn?"*

*"I'll tell you about Flinn,"* the colonel promptly rejoined. *"Flinn is as stout a champion of popular liberty as exists. I want to give you your full answer. Flinn came to me last April or March; I had never known him before. He told me he was going to support me, for he believed that this country would not be a good place for his children to live in unless such social and economic justice was done as to make it a good place for other people's children to live in."*

*"He told me that it was a long experience, and he said he needed to learn it, and that he had learned it — had been taught that the safety of our government lay in making the people real, and not merely nominal, rulers of their own governmental agencies. He fought his fight squarely on that issue, and he carried Pennsylvania, and under his lead Pennsylvania*

*adopted a progressive platform – a platform declaring in the most unequivocal terms for direct primaries, initiative and referendum, for every point of the national Progressive platform. A boss whose action is to put in the hands of the people of his state supreme power over him and every other boss is not much of a boss."*

Undated photo of the Flinn family; Senator and Mrs. Flinn are seated at the center of the photo. Photo courtesy of Hartwood archives.

Senator Flinn and Teddy Roosevelt stumping for the war effort in the Oakland Section of Pittsburgh on July 25, 1917. Photo courtesy of and copyright Brady Stewart Studio, Inc.

In 1904 after Senator Flinn's political career was over he retired to Beechwood Farms, located in the suburb of Fox Chapel on Dorseyville Road near Pittsburgh. Senator Flinn purchased the property that contained 350 acres and became a gentleman farmer, raising prize-winning Guernsey cattle, Flemish giant hares, pedigreed chickens, and German Shepard police dogs. The farm sold milk to the local residents (known as Beechwood Farms Dairy Golden Guernsey Milk) and would later supply milk to most of the residents in the north hills of Pittsburgh and surrounding areas.

Senator Flinn also built a mansion on the Beechwood property at 611 Dorseyville Road; this currently serves as a private residence and is not a part of the Beechwood nature preserve. Mary Lawrence loved to grow flowers at Beechwood and to donate them to local causes. In 1920 Senator Flinn gave the farm to his son Ralph and daughter-in-law Jessie Flinn.

Beechwood Farms has been the headquarters to the Audubon Society of Western Pennsylvania since 1977.

Beechwood Farms today. Photo courtesy of the author.

Undated photo of an old truck in front of a barn at Beechwood Farms. Photo courtesy of the Audubon Society of Western PA.

Farm hands from Beechwood Farms. Undated photo courtesy of the Audubon Society of Western PA.

Undated photo of Beechwood Farms, about the time it was owned by Senator Flinn. Photo courtesy of the Audubon Society of Western PA.

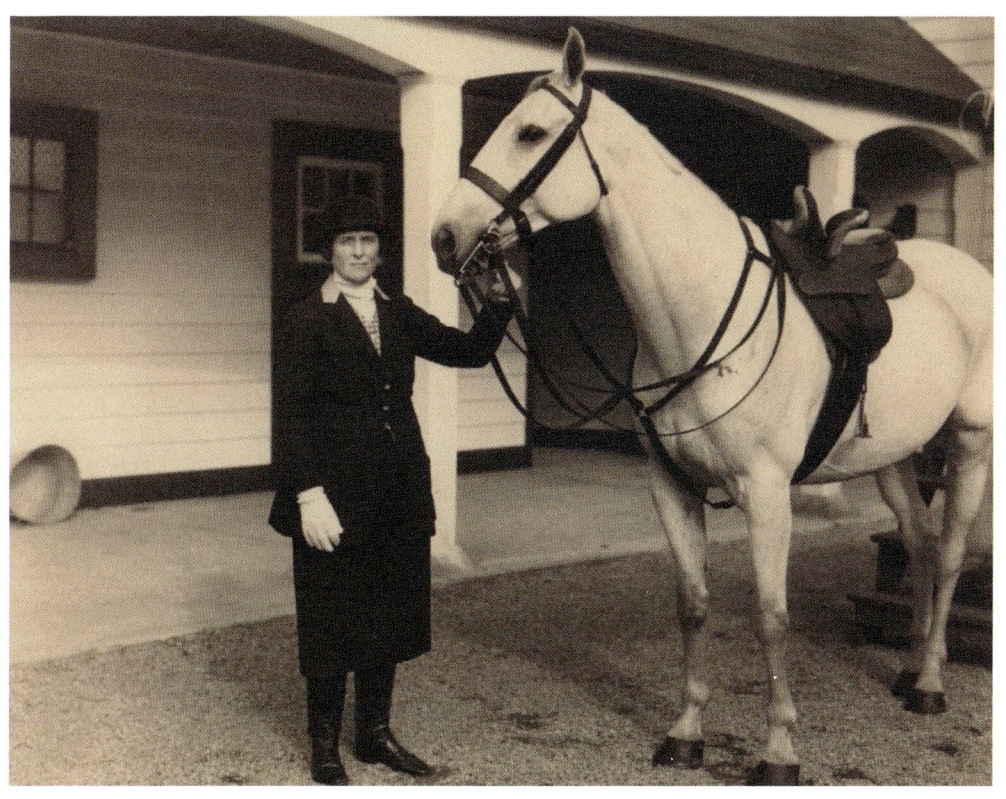

Undated photo of a Flinn family member and the stables at Beechwood Farms. Photo courtesy of Hartwood archives.

Nancy Louise Patterson (daughter of Edith Flinn Patterson) riding a pony at Beechwood Farms. Photo from undated family home movie and courtesy of the author.

Senator Flinn passed away at the Hotel Soreno in St. Petersburg, Florida on February 19, 1924 of bronchial pneumonia. He and his wife frequently wintered in Florida due the Senator's health issues. At the time of his death the Senator and his wife were at the hotel to plan their 50th wedding anniversary celebration. After his passing, Senator Flinn's body arrived by railroad at the East Liberty Station of the Pennsylvania Railroad; he was taken to his mansion called "Braemar" at 1455 North Highland Avenue in the East Liberty section of Pittsburgh to lie in state until his funeral on February 23, 1924. Braemar was located at the corner of North Highland Avenue and Bunker Hill Street at the entrance to Highland Park. Braemar was razed around 1930. Flinn's remains were interred in the Flinn family mausoleum at the Homewood Cemetery in Pittsburgh, PA.

In 1934, PA Route 8 was renamed the William Flinn Highway on the tenth anniversary of Senator Flinn's passing. Unfortunately, only the section of road north of Pittsburgh is still named after Senator Flinn. Many of the current road signs along Route 8 are currently misspelled "William Flynn" but are slowly being changed to the correct spelling of the Senator's last name.

Flinn family mausoleum at Homewood Cemetery. Photo courtesy of the author.

In an article from the February 24, 1924 edition of the Pennsylvania *Gazette-Times*, Governor Gifford Pinchot was quoted as saying:

*"The Senators death is to me a deep personal grief and loss. He was one of the boldest, most determined and most effective men I had ever known and his heart was absolutely right. His sound judgment, strong will, and potent influence in public affairs made him one of the great citizens of our state. Both in his public character and as a loyal and lovable friend thousands will mourn him in Pennsylvania and very many other states. He was a powerful man. His loss will be long and very deeply felt."*

The following is a list of holdings and interests that Senator Flinn was involved with:

Pittsburgh Coal Company

Pittsburgh Coal Company of New Jersey

Arkansas Natural Gas Company

Columbia Syndicate

Gulf Oil Corporation

Manufacturing Light and Heat Company

Pittsburgh Maternity Dispensary

Witherow Steel Company

Sharon (Pa.) Water Works Company

Pittsburgh Lumber Company

Duquesne Lumber Company

Freehold Lumber Company

Arkansas Fuel Oil Company

Freehold Oil and Gas Company

Pittsburgh Chamber of Commerce

"Employees Association of Flinn Interests" (group of Flinn employees)

Duquesne Club

Union Club

Oakmont Country Club

Pittsburgh Field Club

Country Club of Pittsburgh

Member of the Sixth United Presbyterian Church.

# John and Mary Flinn Lawrence:
# In the Beginning

John W. Lawrence and Mary Stephen Flinn began their courtship sometime in 1910. He was from a working class family from Pittsburgh, she was from an elite and politically influential family also from Pittsburgh. It is thought that Senator Flinn tried to discourage their courtship because of their age difference as well as being from different social classes. John Lawrence was 20 years old and Mary Stephen Flinn was 24 years old.

John and Mary Stephen Flinn around the time they were married. Photo courtesy Hartwood archives.

John and Mary Stephen Flinn with John's mother, Anna Oden Hagerty Lawrence, sometime around the time of their marriage in 1914. Photo courtesy Hartwood archives.

John and Mary announced their engagement at Senator Flinn's Pittsburgh mansion Braemar on March 23, 1914. Their engagement was soon followed by their wedding on June 11, 1914 at the Sixth United Presbyterian Church on North Highland Avenue in Pittsburgh. The Reverend Samuel McCall of Philadelphia and the Reverend A. R. Robinson officiated. Edward Napier played "The Voice That Breathed Over Eden" as guests and family entered the church. "In Paradisium" was played during the service. It was a double ring ceremony. John was 24 years old and Mary was 28 years old on their wedding day. The flowers were from Beechwood Farms. In later years Mary would grow flowers at Beechwood to be used for many charitable events.

Mary Stephen Flinn engagement photo. Photo courtesy of Hartwood archives.

The following describes the wedding party, who they were and what they wore. This gives an insight into the wedding as well as one of the most important social highlights of that year. The Pittsburgh newspapers covered this wedding in great detail and offered the following account:

Miss Edith Flinn was Mary's sister and Maid of Honor, she wore rose chiffon and with a large hat.

John's brother Harry Lawrence was the Best Man.

Mrs. W. Arthur Flinn, Mary's sister in law and Matron of Honor, wore turquoise blue crepe trimmed in red roses.

Miss Mildred Murphy of Chicago and Mrs. George Greer of Collidge, both wore orchid chiffon and lilac hats trimmed in orchids.

Mrs. Florance Harper and Mrs. Jerome Belden both wore pale green chiffon with hats trimmed in apple blossoms.

Miss Lydia Electra Harper and Mrs. John Hall wore corn colored frocks and hats trimmed in yellow roses.

John's mother Anna Hagerty Lawrence wore a dress of white lace.

There were two flower girls that attended, they each wore cream lace and chiffon and carried leghorn hats filled with garden flowers.

Formal wedding day photo of John and Mary Lawrence. Photo courtesy of Hartwood archives.

Bridal table. Photo courtesy of Hartwood archives.

Newlyweds John W. Lawrence and Mary Flinn Lawrence at their bridal table. Note the white marble fountain on the table; this fountain can still be seen in the connecting hall on tours of the mansion. Photo from family home movies courtesy of the author.

After the wedding, a reception for 350 guests followed at Senator Flinn's home, Braemar. The bridal table was on the side of Braemar mansion and was built around a fountain filled with Killarney roses and water lilies. The marble fountain that set on the bridal table was preserved and can still be seen in the connecting hall at Hartwood mansion. In keeping with Mary's sense of social responsibility she invited sixteen residents from the Home for Crippled Children to attend the reception.

John's and Mary's wedding party, taken on the grounds of Senator Flinn's home Braemar, June 11, 1914. Photo courtesy of Hartwood archives.

After their wedding reception at Braemar, Mary and John embarked on a two-month honeymoon in New England, stopping in New York to spend the night with former President and Mrs. Theodore Roosevelt at the Roosevelt estate Sagamore Hill. While in New England they also stopped by Mary's brother George H. Flinn's estate in East Hampton, New York for a polo match. They later took an extended honeymoon to the Southwest. The young couple returned to Braemar in Pittsburgh where they would live until 1929 when Hartwood was completed.

Soon-to-be bride Mary Stephen Flinn exits the limo at the Sixth United Presbyterian Church on June 11, 1914. The license plate on the limo reads "Pennsylvania 1914". Photo from family home movies courtesy of the author.

Mary's mother and Senator Flinn's wife Nancy Gailbraith Flinn exits the limo at the church June 11, 1914. Photo from family home movies courtesy of the author.

John W. Lawrence and Mary Flinn Lawrence on their wedding day, June 11, 1914. Photo from family home movies courtesy of the author.

John W. Lawrence and Mary Flinn Lawrence are all smiles on their wedding day, June 11, 1914. Photo from family home movies courtesy of the author.

The Lawrence bridal party exiting the church on June 11, 1914. Photo from family home movies courtesy of the author.

Senator Flinn's mansion Braemar, located in the East Liberty section of Pittsburgh. In January 1929 the property and dwelling were sold to developer Emil Krause for $12,500. The mansion was razed that same year as the county real estate site lists homes on that parcel being built in 1930. Photo courtesy of the author.

Entrance to Highland Park. Pittsburg, Pa.

Early postcard of Highland Park located in the East Liberty section of Pittsburgh. Braemar can be seen on the right side of the photo. This view looks much the same today as it did back around the turn of the twentieth century. Photo courtesy of the author.

# Mary Flinn Lawrence

Mary Stephen Flinn Lawrence was born on February 20, 1887 in Pittsburgh, PA, the first daughter to William and Nancy Flinn. She received her early education at The Thurston School in Pittsburgh.  She then attended college at Briarcliff College in Briarcliff, New York, graduating in 1906. At the beginning of the twentieth century only wealthy woman were educated. Around this time young Mary Stephen Flinn became a powerful political force for local causes as well as for women's voting rights. She was a powerful speaker and used her political force and influence to aid in many political causes for women's health, sex education, the suffrage movement, and children's charities.

Young Mary enjoyed the life of a family that held a high social standing in Pittsburgh society. Her diaries gave a glimpse into her life of privilege; she enjoyed many carefree days playing tennis, swimming, golfing, as well as walking from the family mansion Braemar, located in the city's East Liberty section, to downtown Pittsburgh. Her interests included more than just ways to pass her time, as she had developed an early and keen interest in social, political, and local issues. She enjoyed spending time outdoors and always recorded each day's weather, along with a few remarks regarding her health and her thoughts for each day. Diary entries from her young adulthood reveal that she was quite sickly, frequently sleeping until noon; she was also bothered by migraine headaches and various aches and pains.

Her social calendar included many events with her sister Edith, with whom she was very close and shared a bedroom at Braemar prior to her marriage to John W. Lawrence. She had an immense interest in a wide variety of subjects, and she covered them all in her day-to-day writings: horses, the weather, politics, the suffrage movement, children's welfare, the symphony, the arts, sex education, health issues, gardening and music (to name a few!).

Later in life she became a philanthropist, which was influenced by her wealthy and powerful father, Senator William Flinn, who also supported many causes both locally and nationally.

Mary Lawrence as a young woman. Photo is undated and from family home movies courtesy of the author.

Senator Flinn was particularly active with the Industrial Home for Crippled Children, a charity that Mary became involved with. Mrs. Lawrence sat on the Board for the Industrial Home for Crippled Children for most of her life, and was instrumental in leading fundraising efforts for this organization. Many of Mary's letters detailed her interest in helping those less fortunate than her. Mary wrote in a letter to a friend, "*I love them* [the crippled children] *very dearly, and I go there very often. It's a perfect lesson to me always to see how happy they are with so little and they are all are crippled in some way*" –letter from the Mary Flinn Lawrence Collection, Heinz History Center, Pittsburgh, PA.

Mary Lawrence visits a child in an undated photo. Photo courtesy of the Hartwood archives.

Perhaps one of her biggest achievements in her early life was organizing and forming the Allegheny County Equal Franchise Federation in 1904 at the age of seventeen. This was an organization that was a grass roots lobby for the suffrage movement in the Western PA area. Young Mary Flinn was known as a staunch Republican and supporter of women's voting rights. She worked tirelessly for the suffrage movement in the Western PA area. Her early writings detailed working with several charitable organizations and she was a prolific fundraiser, raising millions of dollars for both charities and the war effort.

Mrs. Lawrence's father, Senator William Flinn, used his political influence to further the suffrage movement, occasionally speaking at the same rallies that Mrs. Lawrence spoke at. She was also a gifted speaker and was much sought after to speak at campaign rallies to advance the interests of the Republican Party.

Mary Flinn Lawrence used her considerable wealth and influence to advance and counsel several charitable organizations including Red Cross (during both World Wars), Home for Convalescent Mothers and Babies (now the Harmarville Rehabilitation Center), Family Society of Pittsburgh, Pittsburgh Symphony, Allegheny County Election Association, Children's Commission of Pennsylvania, Gray Ladies of the World War, Pittsburgh Skin and Cancer Foundation, Pennsylvania Forestry Association, Moral Efficiency Commission of Pittsburgh, Pittsburgh Symphony Society, Fox Chapel Garden Club, Civic Club, Pleasant Hill Farm Society, and Twentieth Century Club.

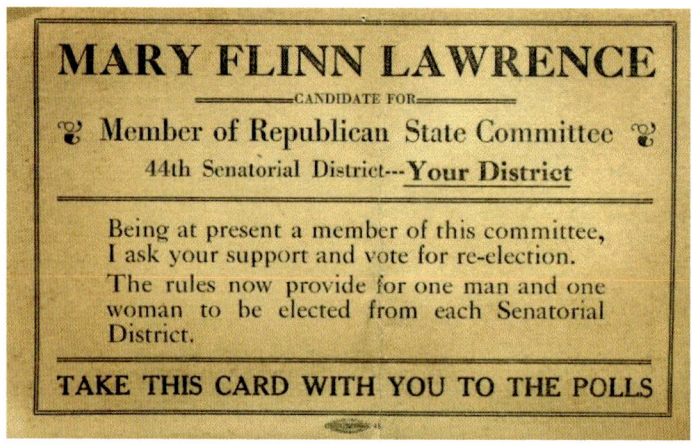

Campaign post card for Mary Flinn Lawrence's unsuccessful run for Republican State Committee. Scan courtesy Hartwood archives.

Campaign post card for Mary Flinn Lawrence's unsuccessful run for Republican State Committee on May 16, 1922. Scan courtesy Hartwood archives.

Senator Flinn was close personal friends with Governor Gifford Pinchot. In 1923 Gifford Pinchot was elected Governor and as a thank you for Mary's hard work on his campaign he offered her the position of Secretary of the Commonwealth in his cabinet. Pinchot served as 28th Governor of Pennsylvania, serving from 1923 to 1927, and again from 1931 to 1935. He was also the first chief of the United States Forest Service. Several personal letters between Mary Lawrence and Gifford Pinchot's wife Cornelia have been found in Mary's personal effects; the Pinchots were close friends and were known to be entertained by the Flinn family at Senator Flinn's country estate, Beechwood Farms.

A study of Mrs. Lawrence's journals reveal that a typical day at Hartwood would begin in her mansion dressing room, having a light breakfast while conferring with her staff to plan the day's events. Most of her days were filled with meetings, fundraisers, or social events. Mrs. Lawrence served on or was involved with countless committees and boards which took a great amount of personal time and energy, which she seemed to be blessed with in her later years.

After her husband John W. Lawrence passed in 1945 she was solely responsible for running the estate and overseeing her employees, which was quite a few during the summer and fall harvest times.

Mary Flinn Lawrence as a Red Cross volunteer during World War II.
Photo courtesy of Hartwood archives.

Mary Flinn Lawrence as a Red Cross volunteer during World War II. Photo courtesy Hartwood archives.

Mary Flinn Lawrence's meeting with the Queen of Romania. Photo courtesy of Hartwood archives.

There were seven finalists including herself for consideration of the Distinguished Daughters of Pennsylvania award that Mary Lawrence won in 1959. Here, she accepts her award. Photo courtesy and copyright Brady Stewart Studio, Inc.

She was awarded a medal for meritorious service from the British War Relief Society. In 1954 she also received their annual Award of Merit from the Pennsylvania Citizens Association. The National Institute of Social Sciences awarded Mrs. Lawrence their bronze medal for "outstanding services on behalf of humanity of social sciences."

Mary Flinn Lawrence and her many dogs. Photo courtesy of the author.

Mary Flinn Lawrence later in life with one of her horses. Photo courtesy of Hartwood archives.

Mary Flinn Lawrence with one of her horses, photo taken at the stable complex and dated 1938. Photo courtesy of Hartwood archives.

On November 7, 1963 Mary Flinn Lawrence was involved in a tragic car accident at the intersection of 40th Street and Butler Street in Pittsburgh. She was returning home from visiting one of her employees who was in the hospital when she was broadsided in the Cadillac that she was driving. She spent the remainder of her days as an invalid recuperating in the cottage section of the mansion. She passed away on October 19, 1974 at the age of 88 years old and her remains were interred in the Flinn family mausoleum in Homewood Cemetery in Pittsburgh, PA.

# Mary's Cadillac

1938 Cadillac Series 60 Special - V8 with a 124" wheelbase; note the spare tire in the fenders. Photo courtesy of and used with permission from myautoworld.com. Mary Lawrence's Cadillac was the exact same year and model in a Dove Grey color; she purportedly traded in a Packer for her Cadillac.

*"The garage held five or six vehicles. In the first bay entering the courtyard was Mr. Lawrence's shiny new 1940 LaSalle Club Coupe. It was light metallic gray with red wheels and white side wall tires. Mrs. Lawrence drove a 1938 or 1939 green "Woody" Ford four-door station wagon with "Hartwood Farms" lettered on the front doors. The family car was a 1938 or 1939 black Cadillac limousine complete with mounted spare wheels in the front fenders, chrome wheel rings, white sidewall tires and chrome or stainless steel running boards with black rubber step pads. Mounted behind the front seat was a rope on which hung a blanket. The vehicles were kept washed and polished by the chauffer Frank Huffman. Between the garage and the entrance to the cottage area was an open shed where the farm truck (initially a black early thirties Dodge stake body with yellow wheels and later a green Ford stake body truck with yellow wheels) surrey, sleigh, and bobsled were housed."*

*Recollections of Hartwood;* name withheld by request.

Recollection of Gerald H. Dumann. Mr. Dumann's father. Howard Robert Dumann was a chauffeur for John and Mary Lawrence in the early 1940's:

*"Mrs. Lawrence never told my dad where they were going; she would just call my dad day or night and say, 'Howard, pick me up at the house.' Dad would not know if they were going to Pittsburgh, a friend's house, Philadelphia or New Jersey. He would pick her up at the house and say, 'Where to Mrs. Lawrence?' She would respond with, 'Just start driving.' They might drive for 15 or 20 minutes before Mrs. Lawrence would tell Dad where they were going. Then she would say, 'We are going to Philadelphia' and Dad would be going west rather than east. Dad was thinking, if I knew we were going on a two or three day trip I would have brought a shaving kit and a change of clothes.*

*When they opened the PA Turnpike there wasn't a speed limit. Mrs. Lawrence always wanted to run FAST. She would say, 'Howard go faster.' My dad said they would pass police officers going well over 100 mph. The police would just shake their heads at him. When he would get around them he would hold the Cadillac on the floor until the engine floated out on top end. Dad said he drove Mrs. Lawrence to Philadelphia and back one time in a brand new Cadillac and then went to the dealership to have four new tires installed. The tires had no tread left on them after that trip. The dealership couldn't believe this car needed tires already. With the concrete on the PA turnpike being rough in texture, all the curves and running at high speeds it had scrubbed all the tread off of the tires. No seat belts, no air bags - just a lot of weight and a big iron motor. The A/C was four windows down just a little and going 100mph.*

*Most of their trips were from Hartwood Farms to downtown Pittsburgh. My dad said he would drive Mrs. Lawrence to downtown Pittsburgh almost daily. The Pittsburgh Press would meet up with them, take pictures and sometimes write an article. Then the depression came along and they started rationing gas, so Mrs. Lawrence bought my dad a motorcycle with a side cart to chauffeur her and save gas. This made headlines when he chauffeured Mrs. Lawrence into Pittsburgh in the side cart. Dad said he liked the motorcycle, but not when Mrs. Lawrence carried an umbrella to keep the sun and rain off of her. One day on the way back to the farm my dad held the throttle wide open until Mrs. Lawrence could not hold onto the umbrella - it was gone.*

*The other story my dad told often was when he was returning from Pittsburgh alone and a guy in a Lincoln tried to pass him. Big mistake he said as he was twisting the throttle open so the guy in the Lincoln could not pass him, came up on a curve that he could not negotiate and ran the motorcycle through a cable wire fence and corn field. He was not wearing any leather and the guy ended up in the hospital for some time."*

# John Wheeler Lawrence

Mary Lawrence's husband John Wheeler Lawrence was born February 11, 1890 in Hazelwood (Pittsburgh), PA to parents Anna Oden Hagerty and Harry Jay Lawrence. Harry Jay Lawrence Jr. was his only sibling. Mr. Lawrence's parents were from the Columbus, Ohio area.

Mr. Lawrence received his education at the Haverford School in Haverford, PA He lived in Bryn Mar, PA prior to moving back to the Pittsburgh area to pursue a career in the oil and gas industries with the help of his father, who was living in Pittsburgh with his second wife. In 1911 after foregoing college he went to work in one of his father's coal mines in Bentleyville, PA to prepare himself for the mining business and to save money for his wedding to Mary Stephen Flinn.

In November of 1911, Mr. Lawrence was hired by the London and Liverpool Globe Insurance Company so that he could establish himself as their local sales agent and later underwrite Booth and Flinn's surety bonds.

When World War I broke out, Mr. Lawrence served as an ensign in the Naval Reserve Air Force. He flew several combat missions in an open air fighter plane wearing the bear fur overcoat that can be seen in the cedar closet on the tour of the mansion.

In 1923 he opened his own insurance firm—John W. Lawrence Insurance. He owned the insurance company until his death in 1945.

John Wheeler Lawrence as a young insurance executive at the desk of his insurance firm. Undated photo courtesy of Hartwood archives.

Mr. Lawrence, like his wife Mary Flinn Lawrence, was very civic-minded and lent his talent to many organizations. He was president of the United Fund in 1941 and of the United War Fund in 1942. He was president of the Fox Chapel Swim Club from 1937-1942. He was director of the Pittsburgh Chamber of Commerce in 1942, president of the Federation of Social Agencies from 1938-1942, and he was also active in the Welfare Fund during that same time period.

Besides his passion for his community service, he was a man with many interests that included architectural drafting, amateur painting, horses, and fox hunting—he was Master of the Hunt for the Fox Chapel Hunt club in 1934. Some of his landscape paintings are still on display at the mansion. It is said that he chose the location of his bedroom in the mansion to take advantage of the sunlight for when he painted in his bedroom studio. He was also an avid sportsman, enjoying football, baseball, hunting, golf, fishing, and hockey.

Mr. Lawrence was also a man of action that did not hesitate to put his life in harm's way for another person: he was a recipient of the Carnegie Foundation Hero Award which is displayed on Mr. Lawrence's desk in his bedroom. On March 22, 1925 while vacationing in Seabreeze, Florida, John W. Lawrence saved Samuel S. Voshell from drowning when Mr. Voshell was caught in a strong undertow 225 feet from shore. Mr. Lawrence was 34 years old at the time. The Carnegie Hero Award is given annually to persons that perform heroic acts. The award is given as either a medal or a small monetary award. The medal that is displayed indicates that he chose his award for the medal only and not the monetary award.

When World War II erupted in December 1941, John W. Lawrence was again called into action to serve his country. On August 6, 1942 he became a commissioned major in the US Air Force, a position he held until his medical discharge from the service on July 5, 1944.

John Wheeler Lawrence as a young man. Photo courtesy of the author.

Commissioned major in the US Air Force during World War II. Photo courtesy of the author.

Commissioned Major in the US Air Force during World War II. Photo courtesy of the author.

Mr. Lawrence was an avid fisherman; here he shows off his catch. Photo is undated and courtesy of the author.

John and Mary Lawrence on vacation in Europe; photo is undated. Photo courtesy of Hartwood archives.

Photo of Mary and John Lawrence in later years; photo is undated. Photo courtesy of Hartwood archives.

Mr. Lawrence passed away at Hartwood on January 26, 1945, from complications of a broken femur that resulted from a fall at his mother's home in Bryn Mar, PA. His remains were interred in the Flinn family mausoleum at the Homewood Cemetery in Pittsburgh, PA.

# The Sons John W. Lawrence Jr. and William F. Lawrence

Johnny and Billy Lawrence at the mansion around 1940. Photo courtesy Hartwood archives.

Many of the docents have said that one of the most popular inquiries that they receive when giving a tour of the mansion is regarding the family. Unfortunately, anyone that lived in the mansion has passed away, but there are many stories about the family that the docents like to share— whether they are from first-hand knowledge or from stories that have been retold through the years.

In his later years John W. Lawrence Jr. (or J.W. as he liked to be called) developed a love for riding motorcycles. The docents loved to tell the story of when they were conducting tours through the mansion when all of a sudden they would hear the rumble of a motorcycle tearing up the cobblestone driveway to the carriage entrance of the mansion. There was J.W., getting off his motorcycle in full helmet and riding leathers. John liked to drive his motorcycle down to Hartwood from his home in Grove City, PA and stop by for unannounced visits. One time, John parked in the lower parking lot and slipped into the mansion unannounced. He then joined a tour of the mansion without the docent catching him sneaking into the group. About halfway through the tour the docent was telling the group a story about John and Bill. Unfortunately, the docent that was leading the group was new and did not recognize John. John was very outgoing and loved to share his recollections of Hartwood with everyone; every so often he would comment on something and share with the group. After a while the docent pulled John aside and said, "You act like you lived here," and John replied, "I know a little about Hartwood." John then introduced himself to the new docent; after that, they laughed and enjoyed the moment.

One never knew when John was going to show up at Hartwood, what he was going to say, or what new story he would share. Everyone at Hartwood really enjoyed John's visits.

John and Mary Flinn Lawrence adopted two boys: John Frederick Scott (his name was later changed to John Wheeler Lawrence Jr. when he was adopted) and William Flinn Lawrence.

Mary became interested in adopting children around the years 1934 and 1935. It is thought that perhaps Mary and John were unable to have children, but this has never been verified. It may be assumed that in this place in their lives—John Lawrence was in his mid-forties and Mary Lawrence was almost fifty years old—that adoption was the best option at that time. Mary certainly loved and cared for children through the various charities and homes that she ardently supported through her philanthropy.

There were many letters exchanged between herself and orphanages in Ohio and the Midwest trying to find children suitable for adoption. The tone of the letters suggest that there was a shortage of children for adoption due to the amount of requests that the orphanages received.

Mary exchanged correspondence with The National Adoption Society from London, England. On October 22, 1937, Dr. Donald Patterson wrote Mary about John Frederick Scott (born June 11, 1934), and noted that based upon his physical exam of the boy, "In [his] opinion, he [was] a fit child for adoption." In the spring of 1938, at the age of four years, John was adopted by John and Mary Lawrence and set sail for the United States. Later in life John would tell the story that he was lucky to make it to the Unites States alive. He would recall that his steamer ship was torpedoed and sunk by a German U boat on the return trip back to England.

Early photo of John W. Lawrence Jr. and friend. Photo courtesy of the author.

John would reminisce about his early life in England before he was adopted. His earliest memory was of him sitting on a curb in London watching a Punch and Judy puppet show.

William was born on July 16, 1937, and was adopted in 1940 at the age of three. John would say that his brother William was adopted from France prior to the war and that he was most likely a French Jew, as many families gave up their children for adoption prior to the war fearing occupation and death at the hands of the Nazis. Details surrounding the adoption of William are not known. It is thought that William did not have an interest in trying to find his birth family. John would recall that shortly after William arrived in the United States William would dive under the grand piano in the great room when he heard planes fly over the mansion.

In 1984 John hired a private investigator to find his birth mother. The investigator found her living in Islington, England. John brought his biological mother to the United States to visit on more than one occasion. She would often recall her life in London during the German blitzes and what she experienced. With a thick British accent she would say, "I would put on me tin hat and blow on me tin whistle" when she heard German bombs falling, as she was an air raid warden for her neighborhood. Almost every home on her block as well as the surrounding neighborhood was destroyed by German bombs; the bombing happened almost every night for weeks and months.

Formal portrait of seven-year-old John Lawrence Jr. - Elizabeth Shumatoff, 1941.

By all accounts, both Johnny and Billy (as they were called as kids) had normal childhoods while growing up. They each had their own bedroom and shared a full bathroom; they were located on the second floor of the cottage wing of the mansion, above the library area. The children shared a butler; his responsibilities included arranging their clothes and drawing their bath each night. Hartwood hosts several weddings every year, and the bride's changing room at the top of the stairs now occupies Johnny's former bedroom. Billy's room was at the left where the Hartwood Manager's office is now located. Billy would say that he would jump up and down on his bed like kids do. He would look out the window and see his mother glaring through the window at him—Mary could plainly see into his bedroom windows from her bedroom. John would say that as a boy he would use a .22 rifle to shoot groundhogs out of the formal gardens from his bedroom window (of course while Mom was not home).

Both Johnny and Billy attended prep school at the all-boys Avon Old Farms School in Avon, Connecticut. John developed an early love of farming from his childhood mentor and surrogate father Lee Eldridge; through Lee's guidance he decided that farming would be his lifelong vocation. In the 1960's, John farmed the Patterson farm located on Middle Road and adjacent to Hartwood, where the Middle Road performance area is now located. In 1966 John and his wife Suzanne purchased a 360-acre farm located in Grove City, PA, which he farmed until his retirement in 1988. John passed on December 21, 2011, in Grove City, PA.

William Lawrence became a professor at West Virginia University in Morgantown, West Virginia. He later retired to the Florida Keys and lived there until his passing on February 25, 2003.

Johnny and a pet raccoon. Photo courtesy of the author.

Formal portrait of John and Mary Lawrence with Johnny in the center. This photo was taken in the mansion library, around the time of Johnny's adoption in 1938. Photo courtesy of Hartwood archives.

Another formal portrait of John and Mary Lawrence with their two sons, Billy (left) and Johnny (right). This photo is one of the author's favorites and is displayed in the mansion Great Room. Note one of Mary's dog's between the boys. Photo courtesy of Hartwood archives.

Billy Lawrence and friend. Photo courtesy of the author.

Billy Lawrence at the mansion around 1940. Photo courtesy of Hartwood archives.

A young and dapper Billy Lawrence. Photo courtesy of Hartwood archives.

Mary Lawrence and John W. Lawrence Jr. around the time Johnny was adopted. Photo courtesy of Hartwood archives.

*"Mom never gave us a penny. I asked my Mom one time for an allowance and she told me, 'I will not pay you for who you are; if you want money you will go out and earn it.' And that is what we did; we learned how to earn money from an early age."*

*"Billy and I used to catch Japanese beetles and sell them to Mom for 10 cents a piece because they were eating her roses. When we sold enough Japanese beetles we went out and bought a Japanese beetle trap. The next time we presented Mom with beetles there were over 400 of them. She then brought a halt to our business venture because she said that we were making too much money too easily."* John W. Lawrence Jr. Personal interview. September 25, 2007.

Photo of a very young future Senator John Heinz (on left) with Billy Lawrence. Date unknown. Photo courtesy of Hartwood archives.

Billy and Johnny Lawrence on cross country skis. Both boys liked to ski the grounds starting at a very young age. One of their favorite places to ski on the grounds was on the sloping yard at the front of the mansion near the hemlock court. Photo courtesy of family home movies.

Bill Lawrence and John Lawrence sharing a light moment at Bill's home in Florida in 2002. Photo courtesy of the author.

# Bobsledding

(From left) Johnny, Billy, Isabel Patterson, and Mary Lawrence driving the bobsled that is being pulled by Blackbird. Photo courtesy of Hartwood archives.

*"I remember one snowy Sunday late in the afternoon, when we would be on our way to the stables meeting the sleigh on the roadway. The sleigh was hitched to a horse and driven by Brownie with Mrs. Lawrence and Johnny and Billy as passengers. At times the snow would be falling and the sleigh bells jingling, creating a wonderful winter scene, one such found on Christmas greeting cards. My father drove slowly by as to not frighten the horse. Once we met the bobsled pulled by a team of horses with a number of people aboard. I believe Lee Eldridge was the driver, my father said Lee was one of Mrs. Lawrence's favorite workers. On occasion we would see the surrey being prepared on the roadway in the summertime."*

*Recollections of Hartwood*; name withheld by request.

Mary Lawrence driving the bobsled near the mansion, unknown date. Photo courtesy of Hartwood archives.

# The Mansion: Design and Construction

At the time of Senator Flinn's passing on February 19, 1924, both John and Mary Lawrence were living at the senator's estate named Braemar, located in the East Liberty section of Pittsburgh. At the time, the senator's estate was estimated to be worth approximately $10.5 million ($10 million estate plus $500,000 in real estate). This dollar amount in 2015 dollars is worth approximately $142 million.

As detailed by several articles in the Pittsburgh Press, his wife Nancy and their six children all received a percentage share of the senator's estate. The senator's daughter Mary Flinn Lawrence received a 16.25% share in trust worth approximately $1.7 million in 1924 (in 2015 this dollar amount is worth approximately $23 million). Please keep in mind that in 1924 there was neither an inheritance tax nor income tax. In his will the senator also bequeathed a one percent share to West Penn Hospital. Braemar and Beechwood, the senator's summer home and farm in Hampton Township, were both left to the senator's wife Nancy Flinn.

Soon after receiving her portion of her inheritance, Mary and John Lawrence purchased approximately 479 acres in Hampton Township to build their new estate. It is thought that the land purchase that would become Hartwood occurred around 1926. At that time it was one of the largest privately owned tracts of land in the county. The tract of land that they purchased originally was owned by the Hart family; it was deeded to Mr. Hart for his service during the Revolutionary War and was part of a land grant made to his family. It is thought that the name "Hartwood" was derived from the original land owner's name (Hart's Woods).

The other theory about how Hartwood was named was based upon the Old English name "Hart," which means "male stag deer." Perhaps putting the two words together—Hart (meaning male stag deer) and Wood (meaning woods)—the couple liked the way these two words described the land that they just purchased, certainly full of woods and deer at the time. It is fun to conjecture about these two scenarios but no one is certain about how the name came to be.

Mary Lawrence would later plant 96,000 pine saplings on the property as a measure to prevent soil erosion. The property where the mansion is located sits at an elevation of 1,380 feet above sea level, which makes it the highest elevation in Allegheny County.

The Lawrences hired renowned architect Alfred Hopkins (1870-1941) to design their estate for them. Hopkins was known as an estate architect and was well known for his style of architecture, which blended both Gothic and Cotswoldian influences. The architecture of Hartwood is based upon the Tudor period of medieval architecture which was popular from 1485-1603. John and Mary Lawrence traveled extensively throughout Europe. It is admiration for this style of architecture that makes it easy to see why Hopkins was chosen as the architect for Hartwood, especially since the Lawrences liked to visit the Cotswold section of England and Hopkins liked to incorporate the Cotswold influence into the design of his structures. Hopkins strongly felt that local building materials should be used in the construction of the estate. This is why Indiana limestone was used for the interior and exterior walls of the mansion and Vermont slate was used as roofing material for all of the structures built at Hartwood.

The blueprints for the cottage section (the first section of the mansion built) as well as the stable complex were drawn up and dated 1926-1927. The blueprints and specifications for the main section of the mansion were drawn up in the fall of 1929. It is not known who the general contractor was that built the estate. It is thought that perhaps Booth and Flinn may have built portions of the estate, but that has not been verified nor is this very likely as Booth and Flinn were primarily commercial contractors known for building roads and bridges and not known for home building. However, contracts have been found that show that Booth and Flinn Construction was contracted to install the service roads that connected the buildings on the estate. Archived receipts show the gravel and other building materials (as well as the labor provided to install them) were purchased from Booth and Flinn, mostly in the early 1940's.

Early photos of the stable complex under construction list "JW Fetterman Company Builders" as the contractor that built the complex. It is not known whether this same contractor built the mansion, but it is reasonable to assume that the same contractor built the stable complex as well as the mansion. The actual dollar cost of the construction of the estate is not known either.

The specifications that were drawn up by Alfred Hopkins offer an insight into the building materials and methods used to construct such a fine residence. The following are excerpts from the architect's specifications dated August 20, 1929:

*"All exterior walls are to be made up of two walls of Straub cinder block, set 2" apart in order to have a continuous air space all around the building. The walls will be tied together using flat galvanized metal ties. Armstrong cork insulation to be applied directly to concrete block bedded in Portland cement. Joints to be tight butted, all to be laid in strict accordance with the instructions of the manufacturer. Limestone (on exterior walls) to be Antique Buff Indiana Limestone. Ashlar 2" thick in varying courses as shown on the drawings."*

Author – The exterior walls of the mansion as noted above consist of two courses of masonry block with a 2" air space between them; this makes the mansion a true masonry structure. The Indiana limestone veneer on the exterior wall is approximately 4" thick, giving the illusion that the exterior walls are solid limestone. There is also a layer of cork placed between the masonry block walls for insulation purposes.

*In gallery, walls and arch to present cottage and door to living room to be of Briar Hill Sandstone color to be selected. Ashlar to be 2" thick with varying courses.*

*Floor to entrance hall, stair hall and second floor landing and floor of gallery to be of Matowee Stone. Slabs to be 2" thick set in cement joints not to exceed ¼".*

*All roofs of slate, same to be laid as follows: On sheathing lay heavy tar paper carefully nailed in best manner. On this lay variegated green slate approximately ⅜" to ¾" thick and random widths. Samples to be submitted for approval. Ridge slate approximately 12"-30" securely set in cement ¼" thick. Use heavy copper nails of proper quality. All flashing of 16 oz. copper, all valleys woven. Roofs guaranteed to be tight for three years and laid only by experienced men. On building paper nail mason lath crossing same at about 5 foot intervals and slate over these as directed. All flashing throughout slate roofs to be of copper. All counter-flashings where necessary in chimneys to go clear back to tile flues. Counter flashings to be lead coated copper. All roofs against walls to be flashed in raglets. No flashings to show. All workmanship to be the best in every way and all roofs must be guaranteed for three years."*

Gargoyle architectural detail found on the mansion. Photo courtesy of the author.

*"Gutters and leaders of sizes shown on plans to be in extra heavy lead covered copper securely fastened to roofs with heavy galvanized iron hangers and to walls with heavy galvanized iron straps covered with lead covered copper bands of sizes as shown. The gutters and leaders except in service court wall will have ornamental copper faces. All other gutters and leaders required or shown will be plain. Fascia for gutters will be cyprus."*

Specifications for the cork insulation in the attic and second floor areas were let on April 2, 1940. This was one of the last phases of the work performed at the mansion. The estate has a working gas well that provided free gas to heat the home.

This is one of the earliest known photos of John and Mary Flinn Lawrence taken during the construction of the mansion. Photo courtesy of the author.

John W. Lawrence standing outside of the mansion during construction, notice his dog in the foreground. Photo courtesy of the author.

Mary Flinn Lawrence standing at the carriage entrance during construction of the mansion. Note the scaffolding surrounding the door as well as the two dogs in the foreground. Photo is undated. Photo courtesy of the author.

Modern photo of the carriage entrance. Photo courtesy of the author.

The rear of the mansion during construction; the cobblestone drive has not yet been laid. Note the extent of the roof scaffolding. Photo courtesy of the author.

The front courtyard area that now overlooks the hemlock court. Note the stone mason in the corner as well as the pile of debris. Photo courtesy of the author.

A local family lodged the stone masons that worked on the mansion; here is their recollection:

*"My family owned the farmer's market at the corner of Saxonburg Blvd. and Middle Road. We lived near the market on Middle Road near the Patterson farm. My Mom fed and provided board for a weekly fee to the stone masons that built the mansion. Mom said that there were usually 5-7 of them at a time and they were from New York, she said that they were immigrants but she was not sure from what country. Mom would feed them breakfast and then take their lunches to them at the mansion on a horse drawn cart."* Jim Giehl. Personal interview. February 13, 2014.

Mary Flinn Lawrence at the front entrance overlooking the courtyard terrace sometime around 1928. Photo courtesy of the author.

Photo of the completed mansion. Note the planted saplings in the foreground; this is where the formal gardens are today and approximately where the dog graveyard is located. Photo courtesy of the author.

The front of the mansion. Note that the cottage section (on the left) had not yet been connected to the rest of the mansion. The cottage section was the first phase of the building of the mansion and where John and Mary Flinn Lawrence lived while the rest of the mansion was constructed. This view is from where the hemlock court now stands. Photo courtesy of the author.

Another photo of where the main section of the mansion is yet to be connected to the cottage section of the home. Photo courtesy of the author.

The front courtyard of the mansion. Photo courtesy of the author.

"The cook Hedwig Sands would park her car in that little garage in the back near the kitchen. She would open up two wood doors and park her car in there." Alan Reed. Personal interview. January 10, 2015.
The courtyard area outside of the kitchen. The small structure at the left was a once a single car garage where the chauffer kept Mrs. Lawrence's car. This small garage was later converted to public restrooms which are in use today. Photo courtesy of the author.

The rear of the mansion showing the front of the cottage section. This cottage section of the mansion is where the mansion tours begin. Note the canvas awnings. They have long since disappeared but metal awning supports that were drilled into the exterior limestone wall can still be seen today. Photo courtesy of the author.

The stable complex under construction. The photo is undated and notes the architect as Alfred W. Hopkins, which is the same architect that designed the mansion. Photo courtesy of the author.

The stable complex under construction. The photo references J.W. Fetterman Company as the contractor. Photo courtesy of the author.

The stable complex under construction. Photo courtesy of the author.

# The Mansion Rooms: Personal Reflections

## THE COTTAGE SECTION

The cottage section is where the Hartwood tour experience of the 22-room mansion begins and guests are greeted. This part of the mansion was the first section built for the Lawrences to live in while the main part of the mansion was being constructed. Groundbreaking for this section was sometime in 1925 and John and Mary Lawrence lived in this section named "The Cottage." This section consists of four bedrooms and two baths. There is a Tudor Rose motif on the plaster ceiling in the waiting area for the tour. After Mary Lawrence sustained debilitating injuries in a car accident in 1963, the cottage section became her main living area. After her accident, the main section of the home was closed off and never used again.

The room where the tour begins was Mrs. Lawrence's bedroom from 1963 until her passing in October 1974. The Lawrences' two sons each had a bedroom in the space above the library. Johnny Lawrence's room is now where brides prepare for their weddings at the mansion. Billy Lawrence's room is now an office for the park manager. Each boy shared a full bathroom that the butler would use to draw their baths. The guest bedroom at the rear of the cottage is now the mansion's gift shop.

John W. Lawrence Jr. shares his recollections:

*"This room was my mom's bedroom. She lived in here during the building of the main part of the house. She also lived in this room after her accident and while dad was in the war. After the accident she lived here bedridden for about 10 years. The nurse stayed in my dad's bedroom upstairs while my mom stayed in this room. It was really very comfortable for her. One of her nurses was named Lombardo and she was from West Middlesex, PA. The names of her other two nurses escapes me right now but we had three nurses around the clock caring for her."*

*"This was my father's bedroom; while they were building the main part of the house they kept this room open. Above the bedroom is a full-size attic with a cedar room, with a very steep stair case—as little kids my brother and I were forbidden to climb these stairs. The tile bathroom was shared by*

*both mom and dad; I used to come downstairs sometimes and use this shower as I did not have a shower upstairs in my room."*

(A linen closet between the library and Mary Lawrence's bedroom):

*"One day mom opened the door and there were 15-20 little snakes in there. They were blacksnakes, and mom took after the snakes with a fly swatter. Mom and I really had words; I told her she was going to kill them and she said that she intended to. She said that they were in her house and that she did not like them there. I then caught the snakes and put them outside. The snakes made her very nervous".* John W. Lawrence Jr. Personal interview. September 25, 2007.

Mansion library. Photo courtesy of Bob Vishneski.

## THE LIBRARY

This room really exemplifies the Lawrence family's love of the hunt and the equestrian lifestyle. There are many silver trophies on the bookshelves that were won by various family members at equestrian events. The fireplace is made of formed concrete thought to be made between 1475 and 1525— this style was commonly found in Normandy and England. It also has Tudor

Roses carved into the corners which is the symbol of Tudor style architecture.

This fireplace held the family Yule log, a Christmas tradition going back centuries. Farm boss Lee Eldridge would find a huge log to become the Yule log; the log would then be placed in the fireplace. The tradition required that the new log be lit from remnants of the log that was used the prior Christmas. The intent was to burn the Yule log throughout the entire 12 days of Christmas. Judging by the size of this fireplace, that was probably no easy task! The ceiling is Italian Renaissance geometrical floral. The flooring is wide plank oak with butterfly notches.

Here is a wonderful recollection from Johnny Lawrence about Christmas at Hartwood:

*"The library was one of my favorite rooms. We had a fire going in the fireplace almost every evening. We lived in this room during WWII as the main part of the house was shut down and this is where we gathered. We had our meals here and the dining table was in the center of the room. It looks about the same now as it did then. The book shelves were always full of books. At the smaller enclave as you enter the room on the right was where our Christmas tree stood every year. We had our Christmas tree there and across the room in the corner was where the train was set up. Brownie and Stanley would set the train up while Lee Eldridge would drag in a Christmas tree. At our home we never celebrated Christmas until Christmas morning. You would not believe that Santa Claus was going to visit us because the day before Christmas there was not so much as a Christmas card out; no Christmas decorations were seen. We would go to bed on Christmas Eve, wake up and come downstairs and the house would be fully decorated. The Christmas tree was here full of presents and the entire house smelled of fresh cut pine. Of course I would then run outside to see if I could see Santa's footprints."* John W. Lawrence Jr. Personal interview. September 25, 2007.

Johnny and Billy Lawrence opening gifts in the library on Christmas morning, about 1940. Photo from family home movies courtesy of the author.

## JOHNNY'S AND BILLY'S BEDROOMS ABOVE
## THE COTTAGE

*"My brother and I each had our own bedroom and we shared a bathroom. For a while Billy and I slept in the same bedroom, but we raised so much hell that Mom decided that was not the thing to do. So she moved Billy into the bedroom on the left so that she could look out her bedroom window and watch him through his bedroom window. One day he put me into a cardboard box and shoved me down the stairs as we were pretending we were tobogganing and he almost killed me".* John W. Lawrence Jr. Personal interview. September 25, 2007.

These rooms are now used as offices for county employees and were not photographed.

Marble fountain used on the bridal table at John and Mary Lawrence's wedding June 11, 1914. Photo courtesy of the author.

The gallery between the cottage section and the mansion. Photo courtesy of the author.

*"The kitchen that is there now used to be the flower room. It has since been converted back to a kitchen for the county employees and docents. It was a kitchen during WW II and this is where we did all of our cooking. This made a very comfortable set up for us. There are all kinds of pictures of us kids and family members as well as the marble fountain that was used at Mom's wedding here in this hallway."* John W. Lawrence Jr. Personal interview. September 25, 2007.

## THE GREAT HALL

Seating area in the Great Hall. The Hemlock Court can be seen through the windows. Photo courtesy of the author.

Great Hall at Christmas. Photo courtesy of Bob Vishneski.

Great Hall. Photo courtesy of the author.

Photo of social event held in the Great Hall. Year is unknown but thought to be in the 1950's. Mary Lawrence is in the center of the photo in the white dress. Photo courtesy Hartwood archives.

Photo of social event in the Great Hall. This photo faces the alcove where the Steinway piano is displayed and the band is playing. Unknown year of photo; thought to be 1950's. Photo courtesy of Hartwood archives.

Fireplace in the Great Hall. Photo courtesy of the author.

*"We called this room the living room when we lived here—it is now known as the "Great Hall." There is a wood lift that runs in the wall between this room and the cellar; I would put Billy in there and run it halfway between the floors and lock it. I would hear him scream, "Help! Help!" Mom would then tear into me about it. The reason that we had a wood lift is because we burned a lot of firewood. The wood was cut 36" long. Lee Eldridge and I would go out in the fall and we cut firewood. We would burn about 15-20 cords of wood a year in this house. It helped keep the house warm."* John W. Lawrence Jr. Personal interview. September 25, 2007.

Tragedy struck when the ceiling of the Great Hall collapsed on August 11, 2005. A tour group had just been in the Great Hall approximately 20 minutes before the ceiling collapsed. The collapse caused around two tons of plaster to crush two Georgian folding tables, several antiques, a Fleming tapestry from the 1600's, as well as to damage the Aeolian pipe organ, Steinway grand piano, and dent the brass chandelier that had originally hung at Mary Lawrence's childhood home at Braemar. The Great Hall was closed for around two weeks immediately following the collapse; this room was the only way to access the rest of the mansion from the Cottage section and had to be kept open otherwise. Tours were still conducted in this room even with a huge 20' x 40' hole in the ceiling. Master plaster craftsmen spent 2 ½ months making new molds that matched the existing ceiling and another 2 ½ months to install and secure the 700 newly formed molds onto the repaired ceilings. Fortunately, after $300,000 in repairs and renovations, the majesty of the plaster ceiling had been restored by May 6, 2006. The actual cause of the collapse has never been determined but was most likely due to the age of the plaster and the humidity levels in the mansion.

Aeolian organ in the Great Hall. Photo courtesy of the author.

The Aeolian residential pipe organ located in this room was moved from Mary Flinn Lawrence's childhood home Braemar where it was first installed. The organ was a gift from Mrs. Lawrence's father Senator William Flinn in 1908. There is a room in the basement directly below the organ that houses the pipes and bellows used to power the organ. As the organ aged, it fell into disrepair; in 2013 the organ restoration was completed at a cost of over $200,000. An inaugural recital was held in May of 2013.

The mahogany Steinway piano in the Great Hall was made in 1901. The piano was a gift to Mary Flinn Lawrence from her father for her sixteenth birthday. This piano was also damaged when the ceiling fell on August 11, 2005, and although it has since been repaired, it is scheduled for extensive renovation sometime in 2016. Photo courtesy of Bob Vishneski.

*"Mom would play the Aeolian organ for us; she was very good at it. She played both the organ and the Steinway. There is a story about the Steinway piano. It is said that Billy and I built a fire under it, which we did— I am not sure why we did that, but we did. During the war the furniture in this room was covered in sheets as this room (as well as this entire section of the home) was not used. Billy and I decided that the Steinway all covered in sheets looked like an Indian teepee; maybe that's why we started the fire under the piano. The fossil table in this room as well as most all of the antiques in this room came from England. There are no reproductions in the house that I know of; they are all original antiques. We really try to*

*encourage people to tour Hartwood. They can really appreciate Hartwood, and it is a really beautiful place."* John W. Lawrence Jr. Personal interview. September 25, 2007.

## STONE HALL ENTRANCE

*"The stone hallway is actually the rear of the house. English homes were built with the front of the home facing the road. The terrace was actually in the front of the home. The ladies room that is off of the hallway has tear drop crystals on the chandelier and has a very art deco feel. This was one of Mom's favorite rooms because of the art deco décor."* John W. Lawrence Jr. Personal interview. September 25, 2007.

Stone hall or carriage entrance, the carriage door entrance from the driveway can be seen on the left. This room has the only coffered wood ceiling in the mansion. The art deco powder room is located in the hall to the right, a favorite among female visitors to the mansion. Photo courtesy of the author.

Stone stairway from the carriage entrance to the second floor. Photo courtesy of Bob Vishneski.

## FORMAL DINING ROOM

*"We had supper in here every night at 7:00 pm. Mom sat at the head of the table, I set at the left, Billy sat at the right, and Dad sat at the foot of the table when he was here. Mom always said that the two portraits in this room were of her two favorite men—the portrait on the left is my Dad and the one on the right is her father Senator Flinn. We have had cocktail parties in here where we had four leafs in the table and could seat 21 or 22 people at this table.*

*"Hedwig Sands was the cook and she laid out a magnificent spread. All of the food was cooked or baked here at the house, there was no catering ever. We had a closet over in the corner that had liquor in it and it was locked. Mom would say, 'If you are going to drink, drink in front of me and not behind my back;' we grew up never craving liquor because of this. The large window at the rear of the room overlooks the terrace, and all of the gold in this room is gold leaf. This room was especially nice with the crystal chandeliers. The fossilized marble table is extremely rare. I asked Mom about this table one time and she said that there were only 2 tables in existence like this; we bought one and she wished that she had bought the other one.*

*"The house has been shot at since Mom passed away. A guy shot a bullet through the window and it went into the gold crown mold near the ceiling. After that the county started putting security on the house."* John W. Lawrence Jr. Personal interview. September 25, 2007.

Dining room decorated for Christmas. Note the portrait of Senator Flinn on the right. Photo courtesy of Bob Vishneski.

Formal dining room, the portrait on the left is of Mary Lawrence's husband John W. Lawrence. Photo courtesy of author.

Formal dining room, the portrait of Mary Lawrence's father Senator William Flinn hangs to the right. Mary Lawrence often said that this room contained portraits of her two favorite men – her husband and father. Photo courtesy of author.

# PANTRY

*"One of the neat things in here is the plate warmer—you put food in it while you served the rest of the meal. The walk-in silver safe is also in this room; no one seems to know the combination except me and I know the combination and I am not telling anybody (laughs). The other interesting thing is the old refrigerator. It is an old GE with the cooling coil on top, it was a great old refrigerator that was built-in which was not common for the day. The sinks in here are commercial grade and I believe they are made of German silver, but they could be stainless, I am not sure."* John W. Lawrence Jr. Personal interview. September 25, 2007.

# THE KITCHEN

Gas stove in the kitchen. Photo courtesy of Bob Vishneski.

*"The stove is a 5 burner gas stove, the oven has no thermostat. If you wanted to regulate the heat you left the door open a notch or two. Hedwig*

*did all of the cooking in here and—my golly all of the food she used to make in here. I came in here one night after a party and I was hungry so I went into the refrigerator. There was meatloaf in there; I found a box of Ritz crackers and ate everything with a big glass of milk. This was around 2:00 a.m. The next morning I came down and Hedwig said, 'Who ate the dog food?' I said, 'What dog food?' She said that she had dog food in the refrigerator and now it is gone. I thought that I had eaten meatloaf but I really had eaten Alpo; it didn't kill me though. I spent a lot of time in the kitchen because I liked the smells."* John W. Lawrence Jr. Personal interview. September 25, 2007.

Kitchen. Photo courtesy of the author.

# COURTYARD

Courtyard where Myrtle Eldridge would hang laundry. Photo courtesy of the author.

*"This is the courtyard area and this is where Myrtle Eldridge—she was Lee Eldridge's wife—would hang the laundry out here. We had it set right in the middle where the drain is now. There was a huge laundry tree that the laundry was hung on. Billy and I used to hang upside down on the gate and watch Myrtle. We would ask Myrtle to sing us a song—she would say. 'I don't sing songs.'"* John W. Lawrence Jr. Personal interview. September 25, 2007.

# HELP'S PANTRY

The help's pantry or dining area. A staff of six servants lived in the mansion during John and Mary Flinn Lawrence's time. A callbox was located in this room. A button was wired to each room of the mansion; whenever a servant was needed, a little flag would pop up with the name of the room where a servant was required. Photo courtesy of the author.

*"I ate almost all of my breakfasts in this room because I was usually up way before the rest of the family every morning. There was an incinerator chute in this room that went down into the burner below. There was also a laundry chute in this room and one upstairs that the linen was dropped down. There is a paging system call box on the wall. When anyone needed anything in their room they could summon help this way.*

*Mom had a parrot that was named Oscar, and he was kept in a cage in the butler's pantry. There was a telephone that was next to the warming oven, and whenever the phone rang Oscar would say, 'hello, hello.' Mom had a fancy party at the house one evening and Oscar was making quite a racket.*

*Mom had someone take him upstairs so that the guests would not hear him carrying on. Oscar's cage was placed too near a furnace vent, Oscar was not very happy about being placed in a room by himself. The guests could hear Oscar saying either 'Poor Oscar' or 'Damn it!' over and over again; that was the night we almost got rid of poor Oscar."* John W. Lawrence Jr. Personal interview. September 25, 2007.

# THE BASEMENT

*"I was told that the foundation walls were a continuous pour of concrete. There were no breaks in it. My brother Bill and I would shoot our .22 rifles down here. One day Hedwig was cooking a beautiful soufflé in the kitchen. Well this same day my kid brother Bill and I were in the basement shooting our rifles when Bill decided that he wanted to shoot a high powered rifle. Bill touched off the rifle, which of course made a very loud noise. Hedwig came running down the stairs yelling at Billy and me because the loud sound of the rifle blast caused her soufflé to fall, needless to say we were not allowed to shoot in the basement after that. We had a wine cellar in the basement; this room with the locked steel door was Dad's wine safe. No one especially kids were allowed in this room."*

*"The basement laundry room, this is my favorite room in the basement. Myrtle would have all of this great smelling soap in this room. She had a big gas fired mangle that she used to iron all of the sheets with. She used a hand iron for the shirts."* John W. Lawrence Jr. Personal interview. September 25, 2007.

# STAFF QUARTERS

Staff quarters decorated for Christmas. These rooms are located above the formal dining room on the second floor. Photo courtesy of Bob Vishneski.

*"The bedrooms at the top of the stairs that led up from the kitchen stairwell were staff quarters. The rooms overlook the part of the field where the horse shows used to be in the back of the house. The bedroom overlooking the hemlock court at the rear was a staff's bedroom. The bathroom is a black and white tiled art deco bathroom. This was the staff's bathroom and overlooks the terrace in the front of the house; Hedwig also shared this bathroom. I did not get up to these rooms very often when I lived here. The bedroom across from the linen room was Hedwig's bedroom. The room looks pretty much the same now as when she lived here."* John W. Lawrence Jr. Personal interview. September 25, 2007.

# *LINEN ROOM*

The linen room located across from the staff quarters. Photo courtesy of the author.

*"The linen room overlooks the terrace and the hemlock court at the front of the house. This is the room where papers were wrapped, ironing was done and various odds and ends were taken care of. The boot black room (located outside of the linen room) was where every Sunday Brownie would take the boots or shoes to be worn to church and would polish and clean them. He would replace laces as needed and was in charge of the family shoes. He was really good at leather and making shoes shine."* John W. Lawrence Jr. Personal interview. September 25, 2007.

# CEDAR CLOSET

Cedar closet. Photo courtesy of Bob Vishneski.

Note the bear skin jacket in the center background. John Lawrence wore this jacket while flying in the Naval Reserve Force in World War I.

*"Both Mom and Dad would have their clothes hanging in here. The black bear skin jacket that my dad wore in WWI hangs in there."* John W. Lawrence Jr. Personal interview. September 25, 2007.

John Lawrence's bathroom – *"Dad had a tile shower with a showerhead with 7 outlets on it – my mom used to call it the 'person's carwash.' This was dad's bathroom as opposed to mom's bathroom."* John W. Lawrence Jr. Personal interview. September 25, 2007. Photo courtesy of the author.

John Lawrence's bedroom decorated for Christmas. Photo courtesy of Bob Vishneski.

*"The first thing you see is Dad's Carnegie Hero medal on the table. Dad was a painter and he used this room to capture both the morning and evening sunlight for his painting."* John W. Lawrence Jr. Personal interview. September 25, 2007. Photo courtesy of the author.

*"There is a bed warmer which is not very common. The reading light is still on Dad's bed; it is a rope bed that had to be pulled tight once in a while after the ropes would loosen. Have you heard the expression 'Sleep tight and don't let the bed bugs bite?' The saying was referring to keeping the bed ropes pulled tight for a good night's sleep."* John W. Lawrence Jr. Personal interview. September 25, 2007. Photo courtesy of the author.

John Lawrence's dressing area. Photo courtesy of the author.

John Lawrence's writing desk. Photo courtesy of Bob Vishneski.

# MARY LAWRENCE'S ROOM

Mary Flinn Lawrence's bedroom. Photo courtesy of Bob Vishneski.

Mary Lawrence's writing desk. Photo courtesy of Bob Vishneski.

Mary Flinn Lawrence's room. Photo courtesy of Bob Vishneski.

*"The room is about the same as when she passed away. The furniture has been rearranged, but the furniture in the room was the furniture that had always been in here. The wallpaper is rice paper which has since been restored by being hand painted. There is a wall safe on the left hand side as you pass from the bedroom to the dressing area. Mom kept Dad's Colt .38 Special service revolver in there from when he was a constable in Fox Chapel. She always told people that if anyone came in her house she could get a shot off at them as they went down the driveway, and it scared me because she probably would have if given the chance (laughs)."* John W. Lawrence Jr. Personal interview. September 25, 2007.

Mary Lawrence's dressing area decorated for Christmas. Photo courtesy of Bob Vishneski.

*"In her dressing area Mom would usually have breakfast in her bedroom on a table and her favorite dog would be in there with her. Sometimes she had breakfast in her dressing area, depending on what was happening that day. She favored Welsh Terriers and they were always a constant presence with Mom."* John W. Lawrence Jr. Personal interview. September 25, 2007.

Mary Flinn Lawrence's desk and office area. Here she would meet with staff and plan her day's events. Photo courtesy of the author.

Mary Flinn Lawrence's bathroom with marble tub. Photo courtesy of Bob Vishneski.

*"The bathtub is marble and I think that it was my Uncle Rex (Flinn) that had a tub like this one. Uncle Rex liked to read in the tub. One night he fell asleep with the book in his hand while in the tub. The book had a bright red binder on it. He awoke to find the water was red like blood and he screamed, 'I have been stabbed!' Needless to say that story was remembered for quite some time."* John W. Lawrence Jr. Personal interview. September 25, 2007.

Front stairwell outside of Mary Flinn Lawrence's bedroom suite. The stained glass windows contain the family crests of the Lawrence, Galbraith, and Flinn families and were made by the Hunt Glass Company of Pittsburgh.

The Galbraith family crest contains the Latin phrase "Ab Obice Saevior," which translates to "Stronger When Opposed." The Lawrence family crest contains the Latin phrase "Quaero Invenio" which translates to "I seek I find." Photo courtesy of the author.

# Hartwood Grounds and Formal Gardens

In the day, Hartwood was a busy place that kept many staff attending to the buildings and grounds. The farmland and the adjacent property and grounds comprised more than 600 acres, making it one of the largest private residences in not only Hampton Township but in Allegheny County as well.

Here is some insight into what a typical day at Hartwood was like as told by some people that worked at Hartwood:

*"Our family became good friends with David Swaney and his family. David became the gardener for the estate around 1940 and his family resided in the gate house at Saxonburg Blvd. The grounds around the mansion, including the garden, were meticulously maintained. During the summer three or four school boys were hired to assist the gardener with grass cutting and garden work. My father was influential in my being hired the summers of 1943, 1944, and 1945. We worked nine or ten hours a day as well as Saturdays. Our pay was 50 cents an hour. My father worked 10 hours a day Monday through Friday and 8 hours on Saturday. There were no employee benefits except a week's vacation was given the last few years of his employment at Hartwood. In the mid 1930's his salary was $60.00 a month. When he left Hartwood in 1941 he was receiving $110.00 a month."*

*"Late in the morning Swaney would pick the vegetables and fruits from the garden to be used for the meals at the 'Big House' as we called the mansion. On occasion Swaney would have me take the freshly picked basket to the front door where I was greeted by a maid. I enjoyed this because I could peek into the mansion. The basket had to be delivered by 11:00 a.m. each day. A larger basket was used on Saturday as the pickings had to do for Sundays also."*

*"Mrs. Lawrence was a prominent member of the Fox Chapel Garden Club. In June we would load flats of flowers raised in the greenhouse onto the flatbed and David Swaney, the gardener, and a couple of us helpers would take them to the garden club and plant them. In addition to specific arrangements, sizes of the plants and color of the flowers were given much consideration." Recollections of Hartwood;* name withheld by request.

*"John Unterholzner would send me up to the mansion or 'Big House' as all of the staff called it. I would take a tractor up the mansion with a wagon on the back so that I could clean out the incinerator and haul the ashes away to a dump place on the property. One of my other jobs was to take a rag and some window cleaner and clean the windows in the basement, both inside and out. I might spend 2 ½ to 3 hours there cleaning all of the windows at the Big House. I also had to clean out the dumbwaiter at the fireplace as well."* Alan Reed. Personal interview. January 10, 2015.

# Dog Graveyard

Canine grave markers located near the formal gardens.  Photo courtesy of the author.

Jerry's final resting place, Jerry was a beloved Schnauzer and not a faithful employee! Photo courtesy of the author.

Here is a wonderful recollection from a Hartwood employee that had firsthand knowledge about the love that the Lawrences felt for their dogs:

*"When I was about eight years old, my father came home from work one day and said, 'You'll never guess what I did today.' Of course, we had no idea. Each year Mr. and Mrs. Lawrence would take a six week vacation to England. This particular year one of the house dogs died (possibly from food poisoning) the day before their return. Not knowing what to do, the hired help working in the mansion decided to have the dog buried in the garden. Everyone, when questioned about the dog's disappearance, was to say the dog ran away. However, shortly after the Lawrences returned the next day, someone told the truth to Mrs. Lawrence. She immediately called a mortician and the dog was dug up and prepared for burial."*

*"My father was summoned to the mansion and instructed to go to the woodshop and build a casket for the dog. He built the dog casket from cherry or walnut wood that was harvested from Hartwood as they seasoned lumber from many different tree species. The casket was built using a brass piano hinge purchased from Auld Lumber Co. in Allison Park, PA—no other metal was used—mortise and dowel joints, with stain and varnished finish. Upon entering the garden from the mansion, the dog cemetery is to the right. The grave marker reads 'Pal 1924-1938,' the one for which my father built the casket."*

Valiant Pal's final resting place. Photo courtesy of the author.

*"With all of the help and the hours we worked, we still had lots of chores. When I worked at Hartwood I didn't appreciate the grandeur of the place. It was just an opportunity for a teenage boy to make some spending money. One of my weekly chores was to cut the grass and trim around the headstones in the canine cemetery. The markers have been relocated and are now placed in a neat row. The original location had two or three markers located in a semi-circular pattern. The cemetery was surrounded by trees and shrubs; I recall a dogwood tree and forsythia bushes."*

*Recollections of Hartwood;* name withheld by request.

It has been said that most, if not all, of the dogs are buried in coffins similar to the recollection above, each made from hardwoods that were taken from the estate. The Lawrences held a small graveside service for each dog.

There is also a graveyard for horses located on the estate property. The cemetery marker can be seen near the access road between the stable complex and the Middle Road performance area. The marker is a sign that points the way to where two grave markers can be found; they are near a field. There is also a small bench to rest on. Rumor has it that there are other horse graveyards located around the estate but they have yet to be located.

# Formal Gardens

Aerial view of the formal gardens at Hartwood. Photo courtesy of Sally Foster.

The formal gardens at the Hartwood mansion were created as a collaboration between a few noted landscape architects. Around 1929 the mansion architect Alfred Hopkins hired noted landscape architects Nicolet and Griswold, Inc. to design the formal gardens and features around the mansion and stable complex. Ralph Griswold from the Pittsburgh firm of Griswold, Winters and Swain drew the original plans. Griswold's plans were to design the lawns, driveways, features, and even the formal gardens; however, for some unknown reason these plans were never used.

The Lawrences then hired Pittsburgh-based landscape architect Ezra Stiles in 1937 and 1938. The hemlock garden that we see today is a design of Mr. Stiles's.

In 1938 John and Mary Flinn Lawrence hired world-renowned landscape architect Rose Greely to complete the design and implementation of the landscaping around the mansion and the formal grounds. In 1936 Ms. Greely was honored with the distinction of being the first female in the American Society of Landscape Architects.

Hemlock Court. Photo courtesy of the author.

Formal garden at the mansion. Photo courtesy of Joshua Wisniewski.

Formal garden at the mansion. Photo courtesy of Joshua Wisniewski.

The formal gardens with the mansion in the background. Photo courtesy of Joshua Wisniewski.

Formal garden at the mansion. Photo courtesy of Joshua Wisniewski.

Formal garden at the mansion. Photo courtesy of Joshua Wisniewski.

Formal garden at the mansion. Photo courtesy of Joshua Wisniewski.

Formal garden at the mansion. Photo courtesy of Joshua Wisniewski.

Formal garden at the mansion. Photo courtesy of Joshua Wisniewski.

Cottage and main section of mansion. Photo courtesy of the author.

# The Fox Hunt at Hartwood

Photo of hunters and hounds; date and location is unknown. Photo courtesy of Hartwood archives.

Fox hunting can trace its origins back to England and Ireland sometime in the late 17th and early 18th centuries. Fox hunting was (and still is) a sport enjoyed by the upper class of society.

There are few documented stories of fox hunting at Hartwood, other than the memories of local historian and fox hunter Susie Todd in her book *Foxhunting in Western Pennsylvania: A Memoir and a History*:

*"Mary Louise Stevenson (Hackett) also writes about those memorable days at the Fox Chapel Hunt. The Lawrence's Hartwood Acres gave us a pristine challenge to hunt in their gorgeous woods and the many untouched fields. There were stunning hunt teas and breakfasts. The members agreed that*

*these hunting days were the most tolerant, healthy, worthwhile times that any teenager could spend.*

*John W. Lawrence, an insurance broker, was married to Mary Flinn and MFH (Master of Fox Hunt) of the Fox Chapel Hunt in 1934. They had two boys, Johnny and Billy. Mary's sister was Edith Flinn Patterson, who had three children: Nancy, Isabel and Reese. Mrs. Patterson had a lovely stable on her place on Middle Road, filled with show horses and hunters. The Family House Polo Matches are presently held on this property. The Rex Flinns were good friends of my family and we loved going to their house in Fox Chapel to swim. Mary and Edith's brother was A. Rex Flinn, who had a charming wife called Dolly. Mrs. Flinn was warm and friendly with people of all ages. The Flinns had Bill and Mary Louise (Weasel) who were contemporaries of my sister Molly.*

*Ralph Flinn was the father of Rex Flinn, and the owner of the beautiful Beechwood Farms. I find it impressive that the highly respected Flinn Construction Company was responsible for making the famous Holland Tunnel that passes under the Hudson River, connecting the state of New Jersey with New York City. Not only were the Flinns successful in business, they were all ardent foxhunters, including their wives and children. The A. Rex Flinns were good friends of R.K. Mellon and were early members of the Rolling Rock Hunt. In later years their daughter Mary Louise (Stringer, Knapp, Davidson) played a key role in the Rolling Rock Hunt.*

*By 1934 John W. Lawrence moved the hounds from the Flaccus estate to the Carr Stable on Middle Road. In 1935 Mrs. George M. Laughlin, mother of Betty (MacDougall, Douglas) and Rita (Blair), replaced Homer Saint Gaudens as Honorary Secretary. Disaster struck in 1936 when the Carr stable burned to the ground and many horses were lost. My father took us to see the ghastly sight – a horrible memory that remains indelible in my mind. The hounds and the outer buildings survived and somehow the hunt managed to continue.*

*In the spring of 1940 the members held a meeting at the Pittsburgh Golf Club and the Fox Chapel Hunt was dissolved. I do not know the reason for this decision, but in accordance with a former agreement Mr. and Mrs. John W. Lawrence assumed the responsibility of covering any outstanding bills. Present at the meeting were Mr. and Mrs. John DeWees, Mrs. A. Rex Flinn,*

*Homer Saint Gaudens, Mrs. George H. Laughlin, Mr. and Mrs. John W. Lawrence, Mrs. Ralph Lynch, Dr. E.P. Moriarty, and Mrs. Albert Wells."*

(*Foxhunting in Western Pennsylvania: A Memoir and a History*, Susie Todd, The Derrydale Press foxhunters' library, 2003; used with permission)

Correction: Ralph Flinn was the brother of Rex Flinn, not his father (Author).

The following is a listing of the Master of the Fox Hunt (MFH) that comprised the Fox Chapel Hunt and the Harts Run Hunt:

**Fox Chapel Hunt: 1926-1940**

1926-1930 Master: George Paull

1930-1931 Masters: George Paull and George H. Cherrington

1931-1932 Master: George H. Cherrington

1932-1933 Joint Masters: George H. Cherrington and G. Bliss Flaccus; Honorary Secretary: Homer Saint Gaudens; Huntsman: (prof.) John Potter; Whipper-in: (prof.) William Ridley

1934 Master: John W. Lawrence; Honorary Secretary: Homer Saint Gaudens; Whippers-in: (prof.) William Ridley and John Ridley

1935 Honorary Secretary: Mrs. George M. McLaughlin III; Whippers-in: John Beach and Harold Ridley

1940 Disbanded

(*Foxhunting in Western Pennsylvania: A Memoir and a History*, Susie Todd, The Derrydale Press foxhunters' library, 2003; used with permission)

**Harts Run Hunt: 1940-1976.**

Members were Mrs. John W. Lawrence and Mrs. Simon T. Patterson.

A young Mary Flinn Lawrence in her riding attire, jumping a fence while riding sidesaddle. Photo courtesy Hartwood archives.

Here is a wonderful recollection from Kitty Bancroft that describes a typical fox hunt at Hartwood:

*"I fox hunted with the Harts Run Hunt. John W. Lawrence was Master of the Fox Hunt in 1934. In 1934 the Hunt was called the Fox Chapel Hunt until around 1940; that's when the Harts Run Hunt was organized and the Fox Chapel Hunt was disbanded. I did not really start hunting much until the 1950's; it was very exciting, and we hunted on drag and galloped across country, over fences, and had a very enjoyable time foxhunting. They were all drag hunts. I hunted for a live fox maybe once or twice accidentally— accidently meaning when a live fox would cross our path. The hounds were used to hunting drag, so when they kicked up a live fox it was different for them.*

*My father George Bancroft was Master of the Hunt for a few years; Johnny Beach was the huntsman I think. A typical hunting day on a Saturday started around 2:00 in the afternoon, we hunted for a couple of hours, there were two or three checks, or maybe four, followed by a pause in the running and then some more running. There was usually a party at someone's house. That was a long time ago.*

*We also hunted on Tuesdays around 10:00 a.m. or 11:00 a.m. That usually lasted about an hour or so but there was no party then. A typical hunt would cover several farms. It depended on where we hunted, how large the area was. We also hunted in the north-country up near Saxonburg, we also hunted in a few areas between Saxonburg and Bakers town. It probably covered several farms. There were many prominent families that we hunted with. I recall Mary's sister Edith Patterson and we used to hunt on her property, which adjoined Hartwood and where the Middle Road Performance area is now.*

*I remember Merle Brown that worked at Hartwood; we called him "Brownie." He did some Whipping-In and following on some hunts, and he took care of Hartwood. I knew Mary Lawrence a little before she was in her accident, and John Lawrence had passed away before I was old enough to know him."*

Kitty Bancroft. Personal interview. December 6, 2014.

Hartwood foxhunt at an unknown location and date. Photo courtesy of Hartwood archives.

Merle "Brownie" Brown dressed in his riding attire. Photo taken at the mansion's cottage entrance. Photo courtesy Hartwood archives.

"Both Mary (Lawrence) and Edith (Flinn Patterson) hosted fox hunts on their farms, with gentlemen dressed in suits and ties mounted on horseback chasing the dogs over the farms. Mary and Edith both belonged to the Fox Chapel Hunt Club. They never actually chased a live fox, but they brought in a live fox in a cage where the fox urinated on a burlap sack. Brownie, the Stable master at Hartwood (he was also Whippers-In) would drag the urine-soaked burlap bag through the woods on horseback so that the hounds would follow the scent." Jim Giehl. Personal interview. February 13, 2014.

The hunt that Mr. Giehl described was known as a drag hunt. This was the most common type of fox hunt at that time and was commonly used at Hartwood. The drag hunt was used instead of chasing a live fox. After the hunt, the hunters would gather at someone's home, usually the host's home, and would raise a toast to a great hunt. Finger foods and sandwiches would be served and tales would be told about the day's events.

A fox hunting party on a local road, presumably around Hartwood. Photo courtesy Hartwood archives.

Early photo of a Hartwood fox hunt, date and location unknown. Photo courtesy Hartwood archives.

# The Harts Run Junior Horse Show

The Harts Run Junior Horse Show. Photo courtesy of the author.

The Harts Run Junior Horse show was held annually at Hartwood for many years and was quite an important event for young riders. This show ranked as highly in importance socially as the Sewickly Horse Shows. Hartwood held this annual show starting in 1931, usually in June of each year. For at least a few of those years, the show was sponsored by the Fox Chapel Hunt, with proceeds from the show being donated to programs to help the needy. John W. Lawrence was Master of the Fox Hunt for the Fox Chapel Hunt in 1934.

Records show that this was the only junior event that was held in Pennsylvania. For each show there were seven events and two classes of riders: Class A was for riders age 12-16 while Class B riders were 6-12 years old. Loving cups were awarded to the top rider in each class. Mary Lawrence and her sister Edith Patterson were the presenters of the awards and Mary was the Chairman of the Ring Committee.

Susie Todd not only attended this event but was also a participant. Here is her wonderful recollection of this show:

*"This annual event holds wonderful memories for me and for many other Pittsburghers. Besides being an exciting day for young equestrians, it was a social event for which the ladies carefully chose their appropriate attire. Each year, The Bulletin Index, a Pittsburgh magazine, meticulously reported the day. For several years the show was held in June at the gorgeous estate of Mr. and Mrs. John W. Lawrence, called Hartwood Acres, which is now an Allegheny County Park.*

*The special quality of the day was enhanced as you passed the gated entrance and wound up the long, climbing, and beautifully landscaped driveway. The wooded area opened out into the meadow below the stately stone mansion. It was and still is a place of well-kept natural beauty and elegance.*

*The show ring was surrounded by numbered parking spaces and there were enclosures in the woods where you could tie your horse. Grooms held the other animals scattered around the area. Although it was an important event, it was pleasant for juniors, and it lacked the competitive atmosphere of modern-day showing.*

*One year I was fortunate in being able to ride the fabulous Chestnut Prince, who belonged to Johnny Beach. Chestnut Prince was so kind and capable that all you had to do was let him know where you wanted to go and he took care of the rest. It was a special treat to be chosen to ride Chestnut Prince. He was loved by many riders and will be long remembered."*

(*Foxhunting in Western Pennsylvania*, Susie Todd, The Derrydale Press foxhunters' library, 2003; used with permission)

Johnny Lawrence leading Billy Lawrence around the ring at the Harts Run Junior Horse Show. The wooden riding ring was located at the field across from the mansion and has long since been removed. Photo from family home movies courtesy of the author.

Billy and Johnny Lawrence competing at the Harts Run Junior Horse Show in the early 1940's. Photo courtesy of the author.

Johnny and Billy Lawrence (on horseback) showing off their pony. Photo from family home movies courtesy of the author.

A very young rider showing her pony at the show. Photo from family home movies courtesy of the author.

Stable master Merle Brown (on far right) with two young riders. Photo from
family home movies courtesy of the author.

Mary Lawrence (second from the left) entertains some women and their children
at the show ring. The small boy in the foreground on the right is future Senator
John Heinz. Note the Hartwood mansion in the background. Photo from family
home movies courtesy of the author.

Ribbon ceremony at the Harts Run Junior Horseshow. Note Mary Lawrence on horseback. Photo from family home movies courtesy of the author.

# Horse Shows and
# Competitive Equestrian Events

Photo of young Flinn family member outside the show ring at the mansion. Unknown year of photo. Photo courtesy of Hartwood archives.

John W. Lawrence Jr. competing in a horse show mid 1940's. Photo dated September 1944 and courtesy of the author.

Johnny Lawrence jumping Little Red in competition, sometime in the 1950's. Photo courtesy of the author.

Johnny Lawrence riding in competition, name of the horse is unknown. Photo courtesy of Hartwood archives.

Johnny Lawrence jumping in competition at the Hartwood show ring, unknown date of photo. Photo courtesy of the author.

Billy and Johnny Lawrence competing at horse shows mid 1940's. Photo courtesy of the author.

Johnny Lawrence in full gallop on unknown horse, sometime in the 1940's. Photo courtesy of the author.

John W. Lawrence Jr. and Mary Lawrence celebrate Johnny winning the Marshall Cup held at Sewickly, PA in June 1952. Photo courtesy of the author.

*"Brownie taught me to ride on a pony with a piece of sheepskin as a saddle and no stirrups, just a bridle and that's all. No stirrups to hold on; you learned to grip with your knees. He taught me how to ride and I became very good at it. I rode professionally for about 16 years. If you had a horse you wanted to show in the ring I would show that horse. When I won the event the horse's owner would keep the ribbon and trophy and I kept the money. In a day's work of showing horses I could make $200-$300 cash. For a 16-year-old kid that was pretty good money."* John W. Lawrence Jr. Personal interview. September 25, 2007.

Billy and Johnny Lawrence on their ponies mid 1940's. This photo was taken at the stable complex at Hartwood, the horse head fountain can still be seen at the stables. Photo courtesy of the author.

Johnny and Billy Lawrence on their ponies mid 1940's. This photo was also taken at the Hartwood stables. Photo courtesy of the author.

From left Merle Brown, a very young future Senator John Heinz and Johnny Lawrence receiving instruction from Brownie. Photo courtesy of Hartwood archives.

# The Stable Complex and Reminiscences

Undated photo of the stables. Note the straw mats and custom hardwood grain buckets. Photo courtesy of the author.

The stables were the showcase of the Hartwood estate—here is a wonderful recollection of what life was like in the stable area:

*"At the stables there was a mat in front of all of the stable doors. This mat was made from rye straw; Lee Eldridge used to raise the rye straw for Brownie. The longer the straw the better it was used for making the mats. They would gather the straw in bundles and put it on the floor, pour boiling hot water on it then cover it with burlap. The next morning before it became dried out (and it was still pliable) Brownie would take the bundles of straw and weave it into a mat that was started on three strings. Brownie would place three strings out and he used the three strings (or ropes) to weave the bundle. Brownie would also weave what looked like round circles of oats or straw for decorative purposes. The stable was absolutely immaculate and quite a showplace."* John W. Lawrence Jr. Personal interview. September 25, 2007.

"*Morning and evening on Sundays the three teams of workhorses needed fed and stalls cleaned. My father would alternate Sundays with one of the other workers (usually Lee Eldridge) to take care of these chores. He received no extra pay for this. When I was about 8 years old, starting at the gate house, he would put me on his lap and let me steer the car (no power steering back then) to the cottages as they were called then, a distance of about 2 miles. This delighted me and I looked forward to those trips on Sunday. Tending the chores took about a half hour. In the winter I would spend the time in the show horse stable or garage (both heated) or visiting the families that lived in the cottages.*"

"*I recall the show horse stable being so well maintained with its red tile floor, stained and varnished woodwork, hammered black strap hinges on the stall gates, woven straw mats outside the stalls on which to place the hay and wooden stained and varnished water buckets with shiny brass hoops and handles. I knew families whose homes weren't as well built, decorated and maintained* as was that show horse stable."

*Recollections of Hartwood;* name withheld by request.

Mrs. Van Horne and Mary Lawrence at the stables. Note the gleaming feed bucket Mrs. Van Horne is holding. Photo courtesy Hartwood archive.

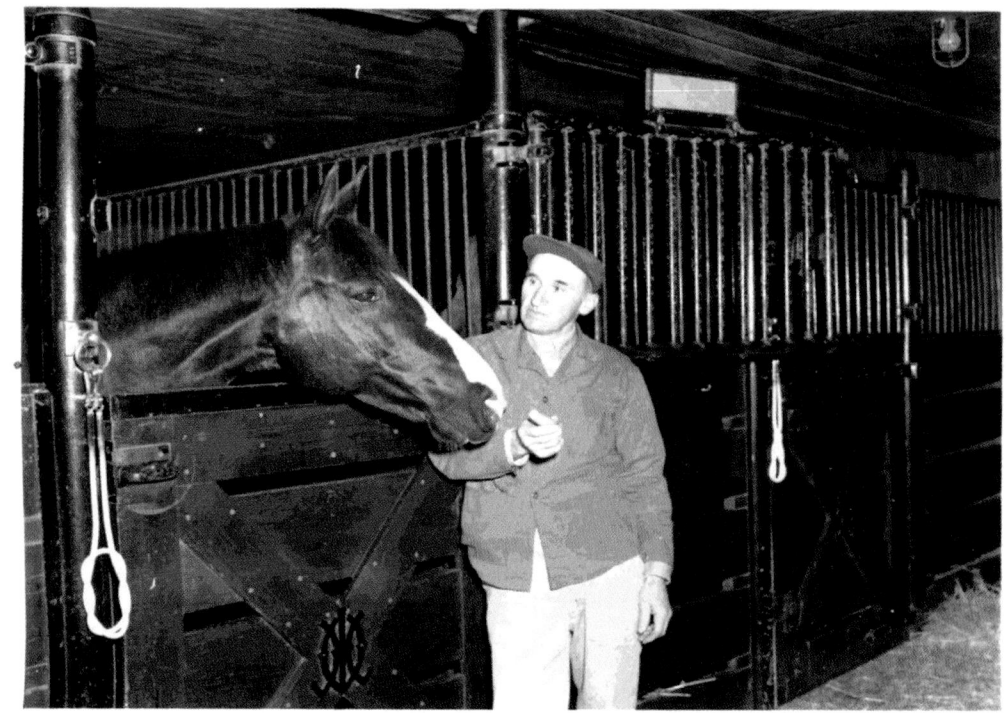

Merle Brown, also known as "Brownie." Brownie feeds a carrot to one of Mary's many horses. Photo courtesy of the author.

Merle Brown was the Stable Master during Hartwood's heyday—here is a recollection of Mr. Brown from a few people that worked at the stable complex:

*"We got Brownie from the Dick Mellon family from the Rolling Rock area around Ligonier, PA. I think he came to work for my Mom around 1947. He was very, very good with horses. Since this was a horse farm he pretty much had a say as to what went on the farm."* John W. Lawrence Jr. Personal interview. September 25, 2007.

*"The horses that I recall are Donnie B and* Wonder Girl*. The tack room had many medals and trophies from the horses that were shown. I was led to believe that* Wonder Girl *was actually a track or a race horse. I also know that some of the horses were used for foxhunting at Hartwood. Brownie put me on* Wonder Girl *one day and she just took off; everyone realized that it was a mistake for me to be on that horse because this horse was running and I could not control her at all. Eventually she slowed down and started*

*walking back to the stables; I was really glad that harrowing experience was finally over because I was scared to death! That was also the last time I got on any horses at Hartwood."* Bob (Bobby) Ladesic. Personal interview. December 7, 2014.

*"The horses in the stables at the time I worked at Hartwood were Donnie B, Wonder Girl, and Dunloe. About the horses—one was Donnie B, which was the black horse with allergies. Donnie B always had saw dust always for a bed, instead of straw. And Donnie B could never eat hay, as Merle Brown fed that horse a mix of oats and molasses."*

*"Dunloe was a brown horse, much as Wonder Girl, and had similar markings of Wonder Girl, and if memory serves correctly, Dunloe was Wonder Girl's offspring."*

*"Billy Lawrence later took Wonder Girl with him to his home in West Virginia. I believe Wonder Girl was a show horse. Merle Brown, I remember vividly, rode Wonder Girl numerous times, just about every day while I would be working on the tractor with John Unterholzner. I recall a couple of fox hunts that occurred on the farm as I would mow grass on a hot summer day in front of the stables. And I vividly remember Brownie riding Wonder Girl in the fox hunts held at Hartwood."* Alan Reed. Personal interview. January 10, 2015

*"The horseman Brownie kept a meticulous stable and stalls, which were dusted a few times a day. The wood and brass buckets were always polished. Even the gravel that surrounded the stable were raked and if you walked on it you had to take a rake and essentially erase your footsteps; it was very meticulous."* Bob (Bobby) Ladesic. Personal interview. December 7, 2014.  Photo courtesy of the author.

Storage garages and private residence at the stable complex today. Photo courtesy of the author.

*"I worked at Hartwood in the late 1960's, in 1967 and 1968. I worked there when I was 13 and 14 years old; it was more than one summer as I recall. Most of my memories are through the eyes of a kid. It was a very interesting couple of summers that I worked there. The main purpose of my working there was not for a summer job but to be with my grandfather and to spend time with him. I remember Hartwood as being a very old place that was filled with antiques, for example there was the Cadillac Fleetwood from the 1930's that was parked in the 10 car garage behind the stables. Also, they had fire equipment that was very old that had to be pushed around on wheels and had a hand pump to pump water. Even the room where we would dress and undress into our farmhand clothes had some kind of old intercom system that went to multiple buildings like the Big House and nurse's house. Everything felt like taking a big step back into time. I came from the city and all of these were strange sights to me.*

*Some of the people that worked at Hartwood were pretty interesting as well. The gardener Stanley called himself 'Frenchie.' He told me a few times he was in the French Underground during World War II, and I don't know if that was ever true. My grandfather John Unterholzner was Austrian born and taught me his strong work ethic. He took over for Lee Eldridge—Lee was the farm foreman and my grandfather was a farm hand when I worked at Hartwood."* Bob (Bobby) Ladesic. Personal interview. December 7, 2014.

The stable complex today. Photo courtesy of the author.

Courtyard at the stable complex today. Photo courtesy of the author.

A peaceful meadow near the stable complex. Photo courtesy of the author.

# The People of Hartwood: Stanley Preston

Stanley Preston at the mansion, sometime in the 1970's. Photo courtesy of Hartwood archives.

Stanley Prostrednik (June 29, 1901 – August 8, 1986) was the master gardener and landscape architect that came to work at Hartwood around 1937. Stanley was known by the staff at Hartwood by his easier to pronounce last name of Preston. Stanley was a colorful person, as we read from the recollections told below:

*"In the fall, Stanley would bring us out to Hartwood to help him smash apples for his homemade apple cider. His wife would make us lunch and it was a wonderful time. We would go to his stone house located at the gate and meet for picnics. Sometimes he would drive us around Hartwood and show off his grounds where he used to work. Stanley had access to the mansion and he would show us around in there as well. Stanley was very beloved by this community. When immigrants would arrive from other countries Stanley would purchase train tickets for them so that they could travel and see the country—I know of at least 6 occasions where he did that. Stanley did not have children of his own.*

*Stanley was very respected by Czech academia. He was from a very well-to-do and educated family as they had a large estate. I think what Stanley learned from Mary Lawrence was the art of giving because giving and providing scholarships is not a part of the Czech culture but mainly American. I don't think that if Stanley had not been involved with Hartwood then he most likely would not have started his own scholarship fund. Mary had a huge influence on him from that point of view."* Maxine Bruens. Personal interview. February 20, 2014.

Maxine Bruens is the overseer of the Stanley Prostrednik Room at the University of Pittsburgh. Maxine recalls that sometime in 1977 Stanley went to visit James W. Knox at the University as he wanted to start a scholarship fund. Stanley was told by Mr. Knox that starting a scholarship would cost a lot of money. Stanley reached into his pocket and pulled out $5,000.00 in cash, slapped it on the table and said in his broken English, "You want more? I have more!" He then went home and came back to Mr. Knox with another $5,000.00 in cash; this became the seed money for Stanley's scholarship. Maxine notes that Stanley's scholarship is one of the most popular at the University as it pays about $5,000.00 annually to students that want to study abroad.

*"Stanley came to us from Czechoslovakia. He was the head gardener for the president of Czechoslovakia. He suffered through WWII in German concentration camps. When he came to work for Mom he never talked about his war experience but I know for a fact that he was captured and put into a concentration camp. Stanley was a Czech patriot and fought in the Czech resistance effort during the war.*

*Over a number of years he developed a strain of roses that he called the "Mary Lawrence"—they were a special color of red-orange and Mom loved them. We have no idea of what happened to them. Stanley lived here after Mom passed away because I told him that if he wanted to stay on the farm he could live in his house, pay no taxes and live rent free in his house the rest of his life. Stanley said 'I am not a slave and you cannot sell me.' I told Stanley that I am not selling him but giving him a place to live if he chose. He was a very proud man.*

*He was a wonderful man and very hard worker. When the county installed the metal modern art sculptures Stanley was fit to be tied. He was furious that the county could install modern sculptures in such a beautiful estate as they simply did not fit in with the architecture or landscape of Hartwood. I will never forget how mad Stanley was when that all went down."* John W. Lawrence Jr. Personal interview. September 25, 2007.

Stanley is on the far right greeting guests at the Hartwood mansion, early 1980's. Photo courtesy of Hartwood archives.

*"Stanley Preston was from Czechoslovakia. He wore this long trench coat and would walk up that long winding driveway from his house at the gate at Saxonburg Blvd all of the way to the mansion with a little Beagle by his side. Every morning he would walk up to work from the gatehouse. He had a little shed near the flower garden where he would grow flowers; it was made of block and was also a tool house. That was Stanley's work area. Every fall Milton Seltzer and Frank Oldfelter would help Stanley gather apples to make cider."* Alan Reed. Personal interview. January 10, 2015.

Stanley's home at Hartwood, the gate house located at the Saxonburg Blvd entrance. Photo courtesy of the author.

The long and winding drive up to the mansion from the Saxonburg Blvd entrance. Photo courtesy of the author.

One of my fondest memories is when Stanley invited me, my mother, and my brother to a picnic lunch at his home. This was in the fall of 1985. Stanley still lived at the gatehouse at the Saxonburg Blvd entrance. He prepared for us a homemade Czech stew; it was very hearty and we ate in his back yard. Stanley had several thousand books all around his cottage; he was a voracious reader and a learned person. Eventually these books were donated to the University of Pittsburgh which became the start of the Stanley Prostrednik Room. Stanley left Hartwood sometime in late 1985. It was thought that he returned to Czechoslovakia but that has not been verified.

Stanley Prostrednik (Preston) at Hartwood, date unknown. Photo courtesy of Hartwood archives.

# The People of Hartwood: Lee Eldridge

Myrtle and Lee Eldridge at their cottage in the stable complex. Photo courtesy of Hartwood archives.

*"Lee Eldridge came to us from Rochester, NY. Lee's first job was in a soap factory. He came to work for Mom at an early age. He ran the farm with an expert hand; he was good with machinery but better with animals as we had horses. Every year at deer hunting time he never objected to me hunting deer on the farm; I know he never liked me doing so but he never objected it. Lee taught me a lot of things about life as my Dad died when I was eleven years old. When my Dad died I was eleven years old; and I became very hard to control. Lee came over to me and put his arm around me and told me, 'I will be your dad; you come to me if you have any*

*problems or anything you want to talk about.' Which I did. Lee taught me the difference between right and wrong, the love of the farm and agriculture, and the love of animals and how to take care of them. He stood by me and we worked well together on the farm."* John W. Lawrence Jr. Personal interview. September 25, 2007.

As my father recounts Lee R. Eldridge (Born 1898 – Died September 29, 1967) had a very profound impact on young Johnny Lawrence's life. He was a surrogate father to the young boy when Johnny's own father passed in 1945. He was so admired by my father that my brother Lee Lawrence (Born in 1968) is named after Lee Eldridge. Lee was well respected by all who worked at Hartwood and left a lasting memory with those who worked there.


*"Mrs. Betty Zbilik was a family friend and was a niece to Myrtle Eldridge. Myrtle told Betty that there was a job opening for someone to mow grass at Hartwood, and this was around April 1964. Lee and Myrtle interviewed me at their house behind the stable complex; she offered me some banana nut bread during the interview. I was hired on the spot and was soon cutting the grass in front of the stables after I got my work permit and physical. I worked a Rhiel power motor. It was kind of like a push mower but it had a small Briggs & Stratton engine on it. I worked at Hartwood from April 1964 until 1970 which is about the time the county acquired Hartwood."* Alan Reed. Personal interview. January 10, 2015

# The People of Hartwood: John Unterholzner

Farm Boss John Unterholzner. Photo courtesy Eleanor Unterholzner Ladesic.

*"My father, John Unterholzner, was a county employee and worked at Hartwood; he left Hartwood and went to North Park to work for a very short while; he then returned back to Hartwood and worked there until around 1972 or 1973. My father started working at Hartwood around 1955 or 1956. When Lee Eldridge passed he took over Lee's position as Farm Boss. My oldest son Bobby also worked there with Father—he recalled he was paid $.70/hour. Bobby was in the 8<sup>th</sup> or 9<sup>th</sup> grade at the time. One of Bobbie's fondest memories was eating lunch in the tack room while working at Hartwood with his grandfather. Bobby said that when any of the horses walked across the gravel courtyard he went out with a rake because the gravel always had to be smooth and perfect. He also helped out with*

*the beautiful fleet of shiny cars, because once a week they needed to be run and cared for. Bobby also helped my father with the cleaning of the furnaces in the mansion—my father always called the mansion The Big House—he and my father would take the furnaces apart and clean and maintain them. My brother Carl also worked at Hartwood and took care of the horses when Brownie was injured once."* Eleanor Unterholzner Ladesic, daughter of John Unterholzner. Personal interview. March 22, 2014.

# Working on the Farm

Field crew baling hay. Johnny and Billy Lawrence play in the wagon while Mom looks on. Photo courtesy Hartwood archives.

*"I worked on the Patterson farm which was behind Hartwood and located on Middle Road. The farm consisted of a white sided farm house, a stable and a horse ring. No crops were grown on the farm; it was just a horse farm. All of the hay and oats came from Hartwood. I would thresh wheat for Lee Eldridge in the same area that the Middle Road Performance area is now, actually in the same spot that the amphitheater is now. This was around 1945-1946. Threshing wheat was terribly hot and dirty work and I remember that we worked fast so that we could finish and head home!*

*The Pattersons had a horse barn in the back along with 15-20 horses in the barn. Mike Fowler was the stable master for the Patterson farm. They also had a show ring and would have horse shows there. The horse show ring at the Patterson farm was actually larger than the show ring near the Hartwood mansion. Both Edith Patterson and her sister Mary Lawrence loved to have horse shows at their farms. Of course Mary had the large farm with around 650 acres. The Patterson farm was much smaller with around 50-60 acres."* Jim Giehl. Personal interview. February 13, 2014.

Field crew baling hay; this photo is a wider view of the photo above. Photo courtesy of Hartwood archives.

A full hay wagon after a hard day's work. Photo courtesy of the author.

*"My grandfather (John Unterholzner) warned me that one of the Lawrence boys was very strong. We would go out in the field and bale hay, which would throw the bales out, and we would have to go and throw the bales of hay onto a flatbed wagon. It was a two man operation, one person was on the flatbed and the other person was on the ground, and he would toss up the hay bales. We use to have competitions with each other; who could throw the hay the farthest, who could throw the hay the hardest; it became a competition with each other in a good natured way. I was always warned not to get hit by a hay bale that the Lawrence son throws because you will get knocked on your tail."* Bob (Bobby) Ladesic. Personal interview. December 7, 2014.

A full hay wagon being pulled to the hay loft. Photo courtesy of the author.

John Unterholzner on the tractor, photo dated November 1963. Photo courtesy Eleanor Unterholzner Ladesic.

*"There was an old tractor from the 1940's and a very old combine that must have been one of the original ones that had to be greased every day before it was used, which took a heck of a long time."* Bob (Bobby) Ladesic. Personal interview. December 7, 2014.

A water break in the field with Lee Eldridge on left and John Unterholzner in the middle; the person on the right is unidentified. Photo courtesy Eleanor Unterholzner Ladesic.

*"Lee Eldridge was getting older and slowing down when I worked at Hartwood. Grand pap and I would go out in the field and cut hay into windrows—my grand pap was still doing physical labor at that time.*

*I never met Mary Lawrence; she was bed-ridden by that time because of her accident. She was called Mrs. Lawrence and the house that she lived in was called the Big House. Brownie kept her horses in meticulous shape in case she did show up at the stables. I did go to the Big House once or twice to clean out some of the furnaces.*

*All of the Hartwood employees were compartmentalized as I recall. It wasn't like everybody did everything; your job was whatever you were best at and you backed up someone when that person was not around. I didn't work at Hartwood for the money, I worked there to spend time with my grandfather John Unterholzner, and money was not the driver for me."* Bob (Bobby) Ladesic. Personal interview. December 7, 2014.

From left - Lee Eldridge, John Unterholzner and Stanley Preston. Photo taken in 1965 at the stable complex and courtesy Eleanor Unterholzner Ladesic.

# A Listing of Known Hartwood Employees

Bair, Eleanor – Housekeeper

Bair, Clyde – Butler and fill-in driver

Barkley, Thomas H. – Blacksmith and stable help

Boyle, Gordon – Gardener, perhaps prior to David Swaney

Brown, Merle H. ("Brownie") – Stable Master from 1941-1974, succeeded William Ridley

Carmel, Ira – Unknown duties, name on the payroll

Charlton, Tom – Unknown duties, name on the payroll

Dumann, Howard Robert – Chauffer in the early 1940's

Eldridge, Lee – Laborer, later became Farm Manager

Eldridge, Myrtle – Lee's wife, worked in the mansion and washed laundry

Graff, Rebecca – Chambermaid for Mrs. Lawrence

Haggerty, Andrew – Part-time butler and cook

Halfender, James T. – Cut grass with a push mower

Holfelder, Frank – Summer help in the garden, worked for Stanley Preston in the 1960's

Huffman, Frank – Chauffer

Unknown last name, Josephine – one of Mary Lawrence's nurses

Keck, Anna Mae – Housekeeper in the mansion

Lewis, Ross – Farm Laborer. Wife Nora, sons Lester and Alfred, daughter Pauline.

Lyons, John – Worked with Stanley Preston as a summer helper

Marshall, Ann – Maid, married to Arthur Marshall

Marshall, Arthur – Butler, married to Ann Marshall

McClelland, Homer – Garden/outside laborer

McClelland, Kenneth – Garden/outside laborer

Nicholas, Joseph Hanley – Butler for mansion parties

O'Grady, unknown first name – Farm Manager in the 1940's, succeeded Bob Powers

Powers, Bob – Farm Manager in the 1940's; son Robert Jr. and wife Martha, also daughters Marcy, Jean and Dorothy

Preston, Stanley – Master Gardener (from the 1940's until Hartwood was sold to the County), lived in the gatehouse until late 1985; Stanley's actual last name was Prostrednik

Reed, Alan – Farm hand 1964-1970

Rhein, Louie – Laborer

Rhein, Clair – Summer help in the garden (Louie Rhein's brother)

Ridley, John – Horseman in stable complex

Ridley, William – Said to be Hartwood's first Stable Master, died in 1940

Robb, Floyd – Farm laborer 1930-1941

Sands, Hedwig – Housekeeper and cook

Schmidt, Marcella – Unknown duties, name on the payroll

Seltzer, Milton – Worked for Stanley Preston in the late 1960's

Slagle, George – Laborer

Swaney, David – Gardener who started around 1940 and resided in the gatehouse with his family

Syms, Mr. and Mrs. – Lived in a house at the stable complex

Unterholzner, Bobby – Farm hand 1967-1968, worked with his grandfather John Unterholzner

Unterholzner, Carl – Farm hand in 1950, worked for his father John Unterholzner

Unterholzner, John – Farm Foreman in the 1950's, succeeded Lee Eldridge

Yocca, Anthony – Unknown duties, name on the payroll

*"Each Christmas the Lawrences would have one of the stores in downtown Pittsburgh (possibly Donohue's) pack a wooden box full of food for each employee. The box was approximately 2 feet wide by 3 feet long and 6"-8" high. Included in the box were potatoes, other fresh vegetables (possibly cauliflower, broccoli, green beans) and cranberries, celery and lettuce. Also included were unshelled nuts, dates, plum pudding, and a chicken packed in dry ice. Just about everything needed for a complete dinner was included. My sister and I especially liked the nuts, dates, and plum pudding."*

*Recollections of Hartwood; name withheld by request.*

# Hartwood is Acquired by Allegheny County

Prior to Mary Flinn Lawrence passing on October 29, 1974, Allegheny County entered into several rounds of negotiations with Mrs. Lawrence's sons for the purchase of the 22 room mansion and estate starting in 1969. The County Commissioners at that time were Tom Forrester, William Hunt, and Chairman Leonard Staisey. The Lawrences were adamant that the estate be sold and maintained as a park for the citizens of the Pittsburgh area to enjoy. John W. Lawrence Jr. entertained offers from land developers from the New York area that were interested in purchasing the property and sub-dividing the parcels into tracts for condominiums. Of course the mansion and all of the other outbuildings were to be razed to accommodate the construction of the new condo units. There was also talk of a Pittsburgh-based corporate entity using the mansion to house executives when in town.

The county initially offered $560,000 for the 629-acre estate. When all offers were considered it was agreed upon by the sons that the best use of the land (as well as keeping with Mrs. Lawrence's vision of keeping the land as is for the enjoyment of the local citizenry) was to sell all of Mrs. Lawrence's land, buildings, and personal effects to Allegheny County as one sale.

The sale of the grounds, buildings, and personal effects of the Lawrence family were later negotiated and acquired by Allegheny County from the estate of Mary Flinn Lawrence at a cost of $1,024,791. The purchase agreement also contained a "life estate" clause that allowed Mrs. Lawrence (and any employees still living on the grounds) to live out her remaining years at the estate without interference. Stanley Preston would live at the property until 1986 when he left and moved overseas. Merle and Alice Brown would live in their home at the stable complex the remainder of their lives.

The only wrinkle in the deal was that the county used the writ of condemnation to acquire the 20-acre parcel which formed part of the former Patterson Farm that was located on Middle Road. It was to be used for a school for exceptional children and was not included in the purchase agreement. This school was later built and opened in September 1971. On this same parcel of land adjacent to the school the Lawrence family retained a cottage and one acre of land as part of the sales agreement. The purchase agreement also stipulated the contents of the mansion and out buildings could not be separated or sold privately and that the family had six months to remove any personal belongings. Hartwood was the ninth and final park acquired by the county.

The Allegheny County Board of Commissioners held a preview showing of the Hartwood estate on July 7, 1976. The Hartwood mansion was formally opened for tours to the public on July 16, 1976. In 1976 mansion admission fees were $2.00 per person over 14 years of age, $0.50 for children under 14, and persons 60 years old or older paid $1.00. There was also a discount rate of $5.00 maximum per family; these fees were charged to help offset the anticipated $50,000/year maintenance costs for the estate at that time.

Since Allegheny County physically acquired Hartwood in 1974 the park has continued to be a great source of enjoyment for local citizens. Hartwood boasts 30 miles of well-groomed trails for hiking, biking, cross country skiing, and walking. There is also an enclosed dog park. In the summer months thousands of people enjoy the Free Summer Concert Series at the amphitheater located on Middle Road. This same amphitheater also hosts the nationally renowned Blues Festival and the Allegheny County Music Festival. Tours of the mansion are always popular; knowledgeable docents take visitors on a guided tour and can answer any questions that may arise. Make sure to call ahead to secure a reservation. During the Christmas season the mansion also hosts candle light tours. These tours will really put you in the holiday mood and should not be missed. There is always an activity that young or old can enjoy any time of the year at Hartwood.

# Filming at Hartwood

The Pittsburgh area has welcomed film crews for the last few decades, and Hartwood is no exception. The natural beauty of both the Hartwood grounds and mansion lend themselves to be natural backdrops to some major (and minor) movie productions.

The following is a partial of some of the productions that have been filmed in or around Hartwood:

- 1978 – The PBS special *A Connecticut Yankee in King Arthur's Court* was filmed at Hartwood; it was produced by the local Pittsburgh affiliate WQED-TV.

- 1979 – WQED-TV again films a movie at Hartwood, this film being their second film named *Leatherstocking Tales*, the second production from their "Classic" series. This production aired on WQED in January, 1980.

- 1996 – A large portion of the made-for-TV film *The Christmas Tree* was filmed at Hartwood; it was directed by Sally Field. In the movie there are some nice aerial shots of the Hartwood estate and mansion. We have a copy on VHS that is watched at Christmas.

- 2006 – The Great Hall inside the mansion was the setting for several scenes for the film *10th & Wolf*.

- 2006 – "Ghost Stories from the Burgh" – Episode One – Hartwood Acres Special Edition - filmed inside Hartwood mansion and tells the stories of supposed ghost sightings of Mary Flinn Lawrence by mansion docents and staff. Produced by 2 Dead Crew Productions. Available in DVD format and is available online and at the Hartwood gift shop.

- 2011 – The pilot episode for *Locke & Key* was filmed inside Hartwood mansion. It was a Twentieth Century Fox television adaptation and was cancelled soon after filming.

- 2014 – Scenes from the movie *The Fault in Our Stars* were filmed at the Middle Road entrance to Hartwood.

- 2014 – While none of the scenes of the film *Foxcatcher* (starring Steve Carell, Mark Ruffalo and Channing Tatum) were filmed at Hartwood, several photos of the Lawrence family were leased to the production staff for the movie. *Foxcatcher* is the story of socialite John DuPont who ran a training facility for Olympic wrestlers at his equestrian estate near Philadelphia, PA. Since both Hartwood and the Foxcatcher estate owned by DuPont were both equestrian estates the film producers wanted pictures showing the equestrian lifestyle.

  Look carefully at the scenes filmed in the trophy room, you will see photos of Johnny Lawrence with his pony. In this same scene you will also see a portrait of Johnny Lawrence with his mother Mary— this portrait supposedly depicts what John DuPont and his mother looked like. There were discussions with the county about using Hartwood for a location for filming. Unfortunately, another Pittsburgh estate (Wilpen Hall located in nearby Sewickley Heights) was chosen over Hartwood for the final filming location.

# Miscellaneous Musings

1. David L. Lawrence – former Mayor of Pittsburgh from 1946 to 1959 and later Governor of Pennsylvania from 1959 to 1963 – is not related to either the Flinn or Lawrence families. Perhaps he and Senator Flinn may have been political adversaries early in his career, with Flinn being a staunch Conservative and Mr. Lawrence was a lifelong Democrat, both active in their respective political parties from Pittsburgh.
2. Contrary to popular opinion, the pet cemetery does not contain the final resting place of any Hartwood employees. The names on the headstones – granted most are human names – are names of mostly canines. John and Mary Lawrence loved their dogs and when they passed they made sure that they were given a proper sendoff to doggie heaven.

## My Earliest Memories

One of my earliest memories of Hartwood occurred around 1972 or 1973, when I was a young boy. Dad, my brother Lee, and I would drive down from Grove City, PA and visit with Mary at the mansion. On this particular day I was trying to catch up with Dad as he was walking through the mansion—he was walking into the Great Hall from the carriage entrance—when I fell down the stone steps leading from the carriage entrance into the Great Hall. I wasn't hurt at all, but it is funny how some memories stay with you for a lifetime (both good and bad). I still look at those stone steps today and cringe!

I remember seeing my grandmother Mary lying in bed in the small room in the Cottage section of the mansion where the tours start today.  It was in this room where Mary was tended to from the time of her auto accident in 1963 until around the time of her passing in October 1974. Due to the severity of her injuries she was not able to communicate with anyone and required round-the-clock medical care. Dad would meet with the staff that was still employed to keep the estate running. Merle Brown (with his wife

Alice) and Stanley Preston still lived on the grounds of the estate at this time. Dad was in charge of the staff payroll and keeping check of the day-to-day work needed to keep the estate running. Dad ran the estate from 1963 until the time the county took it over around 1974, when Mary Lawrence passed.

## Hartwood Acres

Perhaps the reader is wondering why I have not used the term "Hartwood Acres" anywhere in this book. The reason is really two-fold. First, our family has never liked the term since the county named the park Hartwood Acres sometime in the early 1970's when it was acquired from Mary Flinn Lawrence's estate. Hartwood Acres conjures up (at least for me) a name not befitting such a special space. The name "Acres" somewhat cheapens the Hartwood name; perhaps if there were camp sites, water slides, a lake and pavilions on the estate the name may be more appropriate; I am sure that Mrs. Lawrence would never have approved of that name. Secondly, a few sources have mentioned to me that the name "Hartwood Acres" is being phased out. How much of that is true I cannot comment on but I hope it is true. I propose to re-name the park "Hartwood Farms," which would be accurate as it once was a working farm and was the original name of the estate.

# Wicked
# PITTSBURGH

·····················································

### RICHARD GAZARIK
2018

THE
History
PRESS

# METROPOLIS OF CORRUPTION

By the late nineteenth century, Pittsburgh was becoming an industrial ıower. By 1890, the city's mills were producing two-thirds of the ıation's steel and half of all the glass. As the city's population grew, new ıeighborhoods sprouted up throughout Pittsburgh, creating the need or better streets, water and sewer lines, public utilities, new bridges and treetcars to carry people from outlying areas to the downtown.

The political vacuum was filled by Christopher Magee and William ?linn, who together built a political machine by enlisting saloon owners, iquor dealers and grocers who became power brokers in the city's wards. Vlagee went to New York City and studied Tammany Hall. The Magee-?linn hold on Pittsburgh politics stretched from the late nineteenth century nto the early twentieth, enriching them at the public's expense, according :o "The Machine Age—History of Modern Municipal Politics," published ɔy the *Pittsburgh Post-Gazette*. They were big-city bosses at a time when other ırban areas were controlled by men like Boss Tweed in New York City, Martin Lomasney of Boston, George Cox of Cincinnati, Israel Durham of Philadelphia and Abraham Ruef of San Francisco.

The machine's growth was aided by immigrants in need of social and ǝconomic help and businessmen who needed to curry favor with the Magee-Flinn political machine if they wanted to do business in the city, according to Bruce Stave's *The New Deal and the Last Hurrah: Pittsburgh Machine Politics*. The immigrants expressed their appreciation by their votes and businessmen by fattening the war chests of office holders with campaign contributions and bribes. Industrialists ordered their employees to vote for machine-backed candidates or face firing. This combination allowed Magee-Flinn to remain in power. "The machine was simply the political expression of inner city life," wrote Stave, and "reform was a movement of the periphery against the center."

Corruption continued throughout the 1920s and into the '60s as reformers seemed unable to stop gambling, murders, prostitution, voter fraud and persistent political exploitation despite the best efforts of honest men to stop it. Mayor Lawrence looked at vice as the cost of doing business in a big city and tolerated corruption as long as it didn't detract from his political agenda.

Howard Williams, executive secretary of the League for Independent Political Action, told a gathering of city business leaders that Pittsburgh rife with corruption. "I put Pittsburgh down as one of the most corrupt cities in the United States," reported the *Pittsburgh Press* in 1932.

3

# BOOTH & FLINN

## The Company that Built Early Pittsburgh

*Who made the world?*
*God made the world*
*Who filled it in?*
*Booth & Flinn*

choolchildren recited this poem about the politically connected firm of Booth & Flinn Ltd., which played a role in nearly every major building project in the late nineteenth and early twentieth centuries, helping transform Pittsburgh from a city of dirt-covered and trash-filled streets into an urban center.

The story of Booth & Flinn also is a tale of corruption and bribery. The firm prospered through backdoor political wheeling and dealing orchestrated by the infamous William Flinn–Christopher Lyman Magee political machine that ruled Pittsburgh from the 1870s through the early twentieth century. The company became a leading builder in the state and nation until it was sold in 1951 and closed. It reopened in 1961 but closed permanently in 1968, never regaining its former stature.

The Magee-Flinn machine oversaw a period of urban growth that witnessed the development of a downtown, new businesses and neighborhoods, modern transportation, telephones and public amenities such as paved streets, water, gas, electric and sewage lines and clean drinking water.

The success of Booth & Flinn was aided by Magee's cousin Pittsburgh planning director Edward Manning Bigelow, known as "Bigelow the Extravagant," who steered millions of dollars' worth of city business to the construction company, making Flinn very rich. By the time he died in 1924, Flinn had amassed an $11 million fortune. As an engineer, Bigelow wrote bid specifications in such a way that guaranteed that city public works projects would go to Booth & Flinn.

Visitors to the city are surrounded by Booth & Flynn's legacy. The company built the Liberty, Wabash and Armstrong Tunnels and erected the Westinghouse, Manchester and McKees Rocks Bridges along with Ohio River Boulevard. Booth & Flinn drilled a hole through Mount Washington, creating the Mount Washington Transit Tunnel, which allowed the development of the Mount Lebanon, Beechview and Dormont communities in the South Hills. It removed a mountain known as Grant's Hill in the middle of Grant Street, enabling expansion of the downtown area. The company also built Highland Park, where Flinn lived. Even Pittsburgh's cobblestone streets were the product of work done by Booth & Flinn.

In 1895, Booth & Flinn constructed the Apollo Iron & Steel Company in the Armstrong County town of Apollo for steelmaker George Gibson McMurtry and developed McMurtry's utopian community of Vandergrift in Westmoreland County, which was designed by architect Frederick Law Olmsted. When the massive Johnstown flood devastated the Cambria County city, Booth & Flinn dispatched 1,300 men and 280 teams of horses to aid in the cleanup. In 1905, steel magnate Andrew Carnegie built Carnegie Tech, now Carnegie-Mellon University, on land donated by Flinn and Magee.

Booth & Flinn built the city's early water and sewage systems. By 1880, the company had installed the first natural gas lines for Pittsburgh and, by 1895, had begun laying track for electric streetcars. Between 1895 and 1910, the company installed underground utility lines for telephones and telegraph, allowing 30 percent of homes in the city to have telephones.

After Flinn's death, the company continued to prosper. In the early 1930s, Booth & Flinn won contracts to lay the foundations for the federal building and post office in Pittsburgh as well as the Gulf Building. The company was known nationally for building the Holland Tunnel beneath the Hudson River in New York City and part of the New York City subway system. It erected bridges in Rochester, New York, and Nashville, Tennessee, and sections of the Chesapeake Bay Bridge. It also constructed the Bethlehem-Fairfield Steel shipyard in Baltimore, Maryland; the Dravo

Shipyard, Bethlehem Steel, Carnegie-Illinois, Jones & Laughlin Steel and the Pittsburgh–Des Moines Steel Company on Neville Island—as well as sections of the Pennsylvania Turnpike.

By the late 1940s, Booth & Flinn's major clients included the B&O and Pennsylvania Railroads, the Blaw-Knox Company, Gulf Oil, H.J. Heinz, Equitable Gas, Mesta Machine Company, Republic Steel, Standard Oil and U.S. Steel. Booth & Flinn became one of the most prosperous companies in Allegheny County, with an annual income of $4 million.

The company prospered in the late nineteenth century because the city was unable to cope with the massive influx of immigrants arriving in the smog-covered city to work in the glass factories, steel mills, foundries and coal mines. As urban areas developed, so did the need for civic improvements. Pittsburgh absorbed the Southside in 1872. In 1907, it annexed Allegheny City, now the Northside, which boosted the population to more than 521,000. City fathers were faced with decisions about public improvements such as sewer and water systems, new streets and gas, electric and utility lines along with parks and bridges. The development of streetcars created new neighborhoods such as Highland Park, Squirrel Hill, Oakland and Shadyside.

Residents of these new neighborhoods traveled by horse-drawn streetcars to get from their homes to downtown until George Westinghouse founded Westinghouse Electric Company in 1886 and sent an electrical charge a distance of four miles—lighting four hundred lamps in downtown Pittsburgh. The discovery allowed Booth & Flinn to build an electric railway system crisscrossing the city. Flinn held interests in several trolley firms, and Booth & Flinn laid railway track that increased the distance streetcars could travel from 114 miles in 1890 to 469 by 1902.

Booth & Flinn also paved most of the city's streets using a special block that Flinn provided. Flinn saw to it that city contracts called for the use of "Belgian block," which was chiseled out of the Loyalhanna Gorge in the Chestnut Ridge near Ligonier in Westmoreland County, where Flinn owned a stone quarry. When a competitor opened a quarry near Ligonier that produced a similar block, Flinn arranged for Bigelow to specify the stone had to be gray-colored rather than the pinkish color of his competitor's. When Pittsburgh decided to cover its cobblestone streets with asphalt, Flinn went to Ventura, California, and drilled for oil to ensure a steady supply to make asphalt. That endeavor proved profitable for Flinn.

Flinn owned the California Asphalt Company in Ventura, which produced one thousand tons of asphalt a day for Booth & Flinn. He owned 60 percent of the company, while Booth & Flinn, which he controlled, owned the balance.

The Asphalt Trust, formally known as the General Asphalt Company, purchased Flinn's company in 1902, according to the *Asphalt Journal*. Flinn sold his holdings back to the trust, earning $715, 000 in profit for himself. Adjusting for inflation, that figure amounts to $19.2 million in current buying power.

Pittsburgh reformer Oliver McClintock, a member of the Citizens' Municipal League of Pittsburg, charged that Booth & Flinn "did abominable work while charging outrageous prices" for paving streets. When Governor John Tener inspected a street paving job on Liberty Avenue, he was appalled by the quality of the construction.

"The ruts and holes are a disgrace to a great city like Pittsburg," Tener said "I'm surprised that citizens have not sought out those responsible for the frightful condition of Liberty Avenue and taken them to court."

"If you want to be anybody or make money in Pittsburg, it is necessary to be in the political swim and on the side of the city ring," wrote muckraking journalist Lincoln Steffens in "Pittsburg: A City Ashamed" for *McClure's* magazine in 1903. "This is corruption but it is called 'good business' and it is worse than politics."

Pittsburgh was a dismal-looking city during the reign of Magee-Flinn. A visitor could taste the smoke from the steel mills and iron foundries in every breath. "Pittsburgh is a place where the inhabitants breathe, move and have their being in soot and crime," reported the *New York Daily Graphic* in 1882. The smoke was so thick "that a cyclone would only scare the people by making the sun visible for a few minutes." The *Century* magazine called Pittsburgh "the dirtiest city in America." Journalist H.L. Mencken, no fan of Pittsburgh even though his brother lived here and Mencken visited frequently, said the soil of the city was of a particular quality, "being composed of almost equal parts of coal dust, grease and garbage, and is plainly too rich for small plants."

Drinking water drawn from the Allegheny, Ohio and Monongahela Rivers was filled with slag and human waste. The temperature of the Monongahela River sometimes reached 120 degrees because of the discharge from mills. Raw sewage ran into the streets. The lack of clean drinking water in the late 1900s spread typhoid fever, which ravaged the city, afflicting over 5,600 residents and killing more than 600, according to a history of the Pittsburgh Water and Sewer Authority.

From its office on Forbes Avenue, the company employed three thousand workers plus seventy-five clerks. Allegheny County hired the firm to build the foundation for the Allegheny County Courthouse and Jail. The company

The Allegheny County Courthouse. *Courtesy of Wikimedia Commons.*

then shifted to building infrastructure such as water, sewer, oil and gas lines. By 1880, it had installed the first natural gas lines for Pittsburgh and, in 1895, had begun installing track for electric streetcars. Flinn's life was a rags-to-riches story. He quit school at nine and received an education on the streets of Pittsburgh's Sixth Ward, hawking newspapers, shining shoes and working as a bricklayer until his uncle "Squire" Tommy Steele, president of the city council, got Flinn a job in city government and he began his climb to power. Magee studied how state political boss Matt Quay ran Pennsylvania and the machinations of Boss Tweed and Tammany Hall in New York and then applied those same methods to Pittsburgh.

Flinn and Magee formed a political alliance in 1879 that dominated both Democrats and Republicans in the city, Allegheny County and the state legislature—sometimes with a deft political sleight of hand and other times by brute force, according to a 1912 investigation by the *Gazette Times*.

In 1887, Magee and Flinn orchestrated a change in the city charter by transferring appointment power from city council to department heads, whom they controlled. At the same time, state legislator John Upperman of Pittsburgh, a Magee-Flinn crony, introduced the Upperman Bill calling for construction of public works projects "that set the table for a veritable banquet table of public works."

"A political ring can be made safe as a bank," Magee once boasted.

By 1895, Flinn was a state senator and pushed a bill giving county commissioners authority to impose a two-mill tax on personal property to finance road construction. When the tax failed to generate enough contracts, Flinn introduced a measure to give the commissioners power to levy a 1 percent tax on real estate. That revenue would be used to finance construction projects that benefitted Booth & Flinn.

Flinn started a contracting company in 1876 and merged in 1881 with a firm owned by James Booth to form Booth & Flinn Ltd. Flinn was elected to the statehouse in 1879 and to the senate eleven years later. Booth & Flinn was awarded $16 million in contracts for public projects orchestrated by Flinn and aided by Bigelow. Flinn went after government contracts "with a club," steering work to his firm over two decades, mostly for street paving, road building and garbage collection. Flinn once gave a speech on roads that lasted over two hours—even though he had been allotted only twenty minutes to talk. He said public projects were "a labor of love" for him.

"Magee wanted power, Flinn wealth," wrote Lincoln Steffens. "Each got both those things; but Magee spent his wealth for more power, and Flinn spent his power for more wealth. Magee was the sower, Flinn the reaper." Magee and Flinn treated Pittsburgh as if they owned it, said Steffens:

*Magee and Flinn, made Pittsburg their business and, monopolists in the technical economic sense of the word, they prepared to exploit it as if it were their private property. For convenience, they divided it between them. Magee took the financial and corporate branch, turning the streets to his uses, delivering to himself franchises, and building and running railways. Flinn went in for public contracts for his firm, Booth & Flinn, Limited, and his branch boomed. Old streets were repaired, new ones laid out; whole districts were improved, parks made, and buildings erected. The improvement of*

*their city went on at a great rate for years, with only one period of cessation, and the period of economy was when Magee was building so many traction lines that Booth & Flinn, Ltd., had all they could do with this work.*

Thirteen days after his election to the senate, Flinn introduced a series of bills that allocated $7 million of contracts for paving city streets and alleys and the construction of sewers. Flinn's name didn't appear on any of the measures. Instead, he used political cronies to sponsor the legislation, which was designed to benefit his company.

Journalists of the time described Flinn as a "regular old pirate" and a "fierce swash-buckler type with a cutlass in his hand and a lurid bandana wound around his head." Pittsburgh newspapers described Flinn as a physically imposing man, six feet tall, over two hundred pounds, with a firm jaw. He wore his iron-gray hair combed straight back. His managerial technique was a "fist and sledge hammer style," and "no honey ever drips from his tongue," wrote a reporter. Other described him as a "rough-spoken, tactless politician who rode roughshod over political opponents. Magee was the diplomatic of the two patching up quarrels with other politicians that Flinn started."

Bigelow was crucial to Booth & Flinn's success. As the city's engineer and later head of public works, he wrote the bid specifications in a way that awarded contracts based on the "lowest responsible bidder." Booth & Flinn were always found to be the most responsible of the competing bidders, even though its cost estimates were higher. The company once won a contract with a bid of fifty cents per square yard for forty-four thousand square yards of paving material, while a competitor's bid was fifteen cents. In a nine-year period, the firm won 193 contracts despite having higher bids that competing construction companies.

When competitors challenged the bids submitted by Booth & Flinn, city officials couldn't produce the cost estimates that other contractors submitted, so no one could challenge the contract. On one sewer project, Flinn submitted a $138,000 bid, but the final cost of the project was $293,559. City council never blinked an eye and approved the overpayment.

Bigelow was instrumental in developing Highland Park, where Flinn lived and where the city's zoo now is located. Bigelow did it with, and without, the approval of city council. When council refused to approve a purchase, Bigelow simply purchased the property and submitted the bill to city council later. Bigelow personally sold the city ten acres that he owned for more than $1,200 an acre while his wife, Mary, sold one lot for more than $38,000.

Flinn was paid more than $118,000 for fourteen acres. After Bigelow bought parcels of property for nearly $1 million, 30 percent of that amount was paid directly to Booth & Flinn for construction work.

Booth & Flinn developed the South Hills for development by building a shorter way to travel between the city and the South Hills, which was then farmland. Mount Washington stood between the city and the southern suburbs. To travel between the two regions, people had to ride inclines or travel through West End to get back and forth. In 1905, Booth & Flinn built a streetcar tunnel and, fifteen years later, began construction of the Liberty Tunnel, which opened in 1924. Workers cut an opening that was 5,889 feet long, 28.6 feet wide and 16.5 feet high through the mountain of rock. Workers removed 500,000 tons of rock and dirt, which workers dumped at a city park. Pittsburgh officials complained about the disposal and estimated it would cost $100,000 in taxpayers' money to remove the debris. The city sued Booth & Flinn, which settled the case for $20,000.

During the construction of the Armstrong Tunnel, which is under the bluff near Duquesne University, Booth & Flinn crews blasted into the hillside, causing $100,000 in damage to nearby buildings. The company settled the dispute for $16,000. On one project, Booth & Flinn had been awarded a $1 million contract but couldn't account for $410,000 in overcharges.

When two city attorneys were charged with embezzling $300,000 in public funds, it was revealed that a portion of the missing money—$118,000—was paid to Booth & Flinn. Flinn said he thought the money was a loan—which he repaid—but investigators could not find any receipts because they had been destroyed in a fire at the offices of Booth & Flinn.

Flinn spent $121,000 in taxpayers' money to build a road leading from Pittsburgh to his country home, Beechwood Farms, in Indiana Township, where Flinn raised livestock, German shepherds and Belgian draft horses and dabbled in horticulture.

A large mountain of dirt and rock known as Grant's Hill sat in the middle of Grant Street, named after British colonel James Grant, who was ambushed by the French and Indians in 1785. The hump was one hundred feet high and half a mile in diameter and rose on Fifth Avenue from Smithfield Street to beyond Sixth Avenue east from Fourth Avenue to Sixth. Cuts were made in the hump over the years to aid transportation because streetcars and wagons were unable to climb the steep grade. Freight haulers were forced to transport smaller loads and make more trips in order evade the obstacle.

Landscape architect Frederick Law Olmsted was hired by the city to study the problem, and he recommended the hump be reduced by sixteen

The Booth & Flinn Company removed the hump on Grant Street and allowed the city's business district to expand. City council couldn't find the money to remove the obstacle until Booth & Flinn expressed interest in the project. *Historic Pittsburgh Collection.*

feet and the areas between Fifth and Sixth Avenues be widened. "Every delay adds to the expense of manufacturing; the costs being borne by wholesale merchants and the price charged consumers by retail dealers. In short, inadequate traffic facilities add to the cost of doing business and living," he said.

Mayor William Magee complained there wasn't any money in the city's budget to do the work, but when Booth & Flinn expressed interest in the project, Magee suddenly found more than $800,000 in the city's coffers. Critics charged that removing the obstacle would only benefit certain financial and political interests, namely the Mellon family, Henry Clay Frick and department store magnate Edgar Kaufmann. The trio had spent millions of dollars improving their downtown properties and believed removing the hump would make their holdings even more valuable.

A Pittsburgh newspaper wrote that the mayor must be a "magician" to make the money appear. "Mayor Magee of Pittsburg, long suspected of occult powers, now takes his place as one of our foremost magicians," read an editorial. Magee "made the astounding discovery of $800,000 he didn't know the city had."

The hump's removal sparked a downtown building boom. A sixteen-story office building was erected at the corner of Seventh Avenue and Smithfield Street that was known as the Chamber of Commerce Building. The new City-County Building was erected. The Union Arcade was built along with the William Penn Hotel, the Davis Theater, Jones Law Building and three department stores. Booth & Flinn also lowered streets within a thirty-block area. Some older downtown buildings had second floors where basements used to be.

Pressure for reform forced Bigelow to change the method he used for writing contract specifications, opening up the process for more competition. An angry Flinn ordered city council to fire Bigelow, but his brother, Tom

Bigelow, with help from State Senator Matthew Quay, introduced a "ripper bill" that ousted the machine's mayor, William J. Diehl, which ended the political reign of Magee-Flinn. Tom Bigelow became Pittsburgh's new political boss.

Magee died in 1901 at fifty-two leaving an estate valued at $4 million. "When Magee died, I died politically," said Flinn, who remained active in the firm until his death at seventy-two on February 19, 1924. Newspapers had kind words for Flinn, citing his "zeal for public betterment" and never mentioning how he had enriched himself in the process. Flinn had four sons involved in the company: A. Rex, George, Ralph and William. Before he died, Flinn turned ownership over to his sons Rex and George, who changed the company name to Booth and Flinn.

The company continued to be a major force in the construction industry under the leadership of Rex Flinn until his death in 1950. Flinn owned 100,000 shares of stock in the firm, but he failed to make changes in his will before his death, creating tax problems for his heirs—the firm was sold to pay a $3 million estate tax. A New York City construction firm purchased Booth and Flinn in 1951 and closed it. A decade later, it was purchased by former Booth and Flinn executives, but its rebirth would be short-lived. In 1968, the company was placed in receivership and its assets sold. Pittsburgh newspapers noted the company's demise in a short article that said the sale of Booth and Flinn "marked an end of an era."